GW00870229

In Search of My Father's Love

Finding love in the right place

Debra McNeill

Official website: www.debramcneill.com

ISBN: 978-1-4834-6238-7 (sc)
ISBN: 978-1-4834-6239-4 (e)

Lulu Publishing Services rev. date: 12/19/2016

This book I give to you as a gift of love.....

How many of us are looking love?

Man or woman we all need to give love and we all need to receive love.

The challenges we face to find this love will possibly be the most life defining way we make choices good or bad in our entire life time.

If you are reading this, then you have been divinely guided to do so whether or not you believe in God or just coincidences. Reading this book will offer you the hope of finding the true love you seek.

In the words of the song by the late great Witney Houston 'Learning to love yourself is the greatest gift of all'.

Jesus tells us to Love God first then to love ourselves as much as we can, loving others in that same way. Therein lies the key to all of this. We can only love others as much as we love ourselves.

By putting our attention to loving God first, He will guide us into the saving knowledge we need to love ourselves, then we no longer make choices based on our distorted feelings, but on the truth of God's Love for us, and that frees us to expect the best. The best love from anyone no matter what.

You deserve that so do I.

Follow my journey, check out my website debramcneill.com and let's walk together into the best love we can ever experience!

CONTENTS

DEDICATION

To my darling Hugh, with the deepest love and gratitude for your amazing love for me and our family. We are so very blessed to experience your love daily for us and giving to us your steadfast servant heart.

I dedicate this book to you with all my deepest love.

Deb xxxx

FOREWORD

Where are you at? I mean if you were to look at your life right now, where would the arrow be that states 'YOU ARE HERE'?

If you don't know where you are at, it will be difficult for you to know where you want to go. It is only when we can understand where we are at, that we can move forward towards something else.

In the first part of my life, my 'Old Story', you will read about the decisions and choices I had to make and how I chose to live according to the person I thought I was. This will illustrate the limits I placed upon myself because of my lack of vision and not being aware of my true identity. In the second part of my book, the 'New Story', you will again read about the decisions and choices I had to make, but ultimately, these decisions were, and continue to be reached, based on who I am now; my new identity, with a growing knowledge of my higher vision.

In these past few months while writing this book, I came across the most amazing revelations concerning my relationship with my Father God. I began to realise that I was looking for Him from the day I was born, even though, I did not really know He existed for the majority of my early years on this earth. He has been calling me, drawing me nearer, and I in turn, subconsciously to begin with, then intentionally, called and searched for Him.

To begin with, the search was accidental. I didn't even know that I was looking for anything! But God was calling *me* through my circumstances; through choices I made and through choices others made on my behalf. There was no getting away from the fact that God my Father was calling me to be reconciled back to Him. This is what God is doing for all of us on Earth.

At first I was only looking to be accepted. I had always been REJECTED as a child in many ways. But I realise now, that God was using others to be the template to reveal to me what the opposite of 'ACCEPTANCE' was.

God was revealing the true condition of my heart, what the opposite of His deepest love for me was. Rejection. As I battled to find ways to feel accepted I was drawn more and more into the world of rejection. The more I tried to please and behave in a way I considered good, the more I got rejected. The tipping point came when I was at a STAGE OF DESERTION. Everybody had LEFT my circle of relationships, either by their choice, or my rejection of them and I was struggling to stay in that place on my own. The ultimate rejection for me would have been the rejection of me by myself. A plan to throw in the towel, if you like, and leave the life I had been born into. At forty years of age I reached the PINNACLE OF MISERY. This for me was the CRUCIFYING moment of my life. It was from this place of desperation that I cried out to an unknown God,

> "God, if you really exist, you need to prove it to me, otherwise there is no point if after we live, we die, and that is it; finished. Nothing!"
>
> I am reminded here of Jesus on the cross; the pinnacle of his desperation. (Matthew 27: 45-46)

"Now from the-sixth hour darkness fell upon all the land until the ninth hour. About the ninth hour Jesus cried out with a loud voice, saying, "Eli, Eli, lama sabachthani?" (That is, "My God, My God, why have You forsaken Me?")

And, as if to enable me to hone in on the whole business of rejection betrayal, I came across a book recently where the author writes about the Crucifixion and the Resurrection. The main thrust though, is focused on the 'EASTER SATURDAY EXPERIENCE.'

The author allows the reader a thought that JUST AS JESUS experienced his own Crucifixion, we too must receive our own Crucifixion time; a time which leads us INTO THE DARKNESS of our own 'Easter Saturday' experiences. These are the times when life got too painful; where hurts and wounds get BURIED and lie dormant in the darkest recesses of our lives, covered in dust, no longer remembered. Yet the crucifixion time ALLOWS US to look for the lost and the dead; TO DISCOVER the hurts and wounds of our past. These wounds are the ones that cause us to stay trapped in fear, anger or bitterness, or even worse unforgiveness of ourselves and others.

If we are to understand this concept, our 'Easter Saturday' experience follows from our own Crucifixion times and flows into the glorious day of resurrection. Just as Jesus WENT DOWN INTO DEATH on Easter Saturday to release the souls of those gone before, we too begin to eagerly step into our PERSONAL DARKNESS and begin to search for the wounds we received in our own personal Crucifixion. We are able to bring them to the light and give them to Jesus on the day of our OWN RESURRECTION; freedom to give up and yield. JESUS TAKES these wounds and he heals them once for all.

We now carry the immunity of the Holy Spirit that gives us the freedom to go near these once painful memories, whether they are triggered by a personal experience or by seeing that wound in others who are still suffering. We are stronger and can learn even more to train ourselves, whilst using our renewed strength for ourselves and others whom we can support.

To confirm these reflections, it happened that a few days later while I was feeling very low, the Holy Spirit imparted to me a vision. A small brightly coloured delicate bird- the bull finch, sitting on top of a thistly brown dead plant. I watched as the bird, perched deftly on a vertical branch of the plant, and using his minute beak, began to delve into the spikey seed heads and take out the delicate tiny seeds. The Lord spoke and said:

> **"It is only when we die to self that we release the seeds of a resurrection life"**

I died to self on my fortieth birthday and I began to release the seeds of the resurrection life. I began to look into areas of pain from my past and, through guidance and help from the Holy Spirit I found myself surrounded by special Godly mature people, who enabled me to feel safe as I went through my 'Easter Saturday' process, slowly and delicately PICKING OUT THE SEEDS OF DEATH that had for so long held me in darkness. This was, and still is, a process. Each time a situation arose which aroused in me the pain of rejection, I was presented with a Godly guide who helped me to birth into the light, the darkest treasures- a total opposite of what was love but had allowed me to understand from that negative place, the deepest experience of true love; a life my heavenly Father had been calling me and drawing me into over the past forty years. On my fortieth birthday, as I cried out for God to reveal himself I gave up trying to be me, trying to fight for me finding me. I gave up and my Father gently lifted me up and said,

> **"I am here, I will take care of you."**

I realise as I reflect through my writing that God has gifted me with a MINISTRY OF RECONCILIATION. It is well documented that when God gives you a gifted ministry, He will allow you to experience the EXACT OPPOSITE of that experiential life so that you understand and can empathise and encourage those who God then calls you to minister to. Had I not experienced rejection to the pinnacle of desperation I would not have cried out for HIS ACCEPTANCE of me. As I reflect I see and understand the way God communicated and worked with me to point me toward my ministry of reconciliation.

As an example he allowed others who had suffered rejection in their lives to connect with me, through friendships and relationships, living and working in brokenness, a merry-go-round of hurt and hurting because we had not yet received the revelation of Jesus, the TRUE RECONCILER back to our Heavenly Father.

I have rejected, as well as I have been rejected, simply because I had never accepted the truth of who I truly am.

In Matthew 16:15 Jesus asks Simon Peter who he thinks Jesus is? Simon's reply is that he believes Jesus is the Messiah, the Son of the Living God.

Simon has got it! He reveals the *true* identity of Jesus. And Jesus now in return reveals to Simon *his* identity.

> *"17 Jesus replied, "Blessed are you, Simon son of Jonah,*
> *for this was not revealed to you by flesh and blood, but*
> *by my Father in heaven. 18 And I tell you that you are*
> *Peter, and on this rock I will build my church, and the*
> *gates of Hades will not overcome it. 19 I will give you the*
> *keys of the kingdom of heaven; whatever you bind on earth*
> *will be bound in heaven, and whatever you loose on earth*
> *will be loosed in heaven." 20 Then he ordered his disciples*
> *not to tell anyone that he was the Messiah."*

If we RECOGNISE Jesus, we recognise ourselves as being part of Him. The promise is that we now have the keys of the Kingdom. These are **keys of wisdom, knowledge and understanding that come directly from God**. We can call down things of heaven to earth, binding THE THINGS THAT BLOCK US and loosing the things THAT BRING FREEDOM; that allow us to share and live out a deeper relationship with God; that allow us to LIVE ON THE ROCK of the Kingdom of God; being built into a holy house, a huge mansion.

My Father allowed me to be led mostly by my own choices into many dark experiences, but He also RESCUED ME every time, and allowed me to PLUNDER THE GOLD AND SILVER (Exodus 12:35-36) of these valuable experiences, bringing them with me on my journey to use as 'keys' to open the **dark recesses in the lives of others** whom God calls and directs me to WALK ALONGSIDE. I am living proof that even though I travel through times of pain and suffering I AM STILL HERE! I am secure in the love of who Jesus is for me.

As I walked into my reconciliation ministry and away from my rejection, I was, and still am, being led into places that the Holy Spirit can facilitate, through me and in me, all that I can be, to bring about the glory of God in other's lives; a 'SATELLITE NAVIGATION SYSTEM' towards living in wholeness with God. This is my new starting point! I AM HERE!

My new life path has so far allowed me to enjoy reconciliation ministries in youth & community work; families; children; young people; old people; people from all cultures, social backgrounds and gender. I have a great passion for enabling others to reach reconciliation with Our Heavenly Father.

Ironically, my Heavenly Father has now revealed to me who my true earthly father is, **revealing and reconciling a whole new family I did not know existed!**

I am now running towards the fullness of my ministry with wide open arms. I am loved; I am accepted, by my Heavenly Father!

Walk with me through this book, as I reveal how God began to communicate to me from birth, and how through those practical experiences I am able to communicate and grow into the deepest LOVE my Father has for me, for us.

If you are a new follower of Jesus Christ, or struggling in areas of your life, or want to grow more into a deeper relationship with our Trinitarian God, (God, the Father, God, the Son, God, the Holy Spirit), then I invite you into a practical way of living with your heavenly Father and not just being a SPECTATOR.

Come with me and together, let us dance, sing and praise our way into our resurrected life!

THE KINGDOM OF GOD!

CHAPTER 1

The beginning of Hope

Hosea 2: 14-15

Therefore I am now going to allure her; I will lead her into the desert and speak tenderly to her. There I will give her back her vineyards and will make the valley of Achor, a door of hope. There she will sing as in the days of her youth as in the day she came out of Egypt

The vicar was a strange character. He was always distant, yet when he spoke, the wisdom was incredibly apt, especially in connection with my current position in life.

Having gone through the trauma of my husband Stuart's death, I was now beginning to enjoy sitting in the church services. I had initially gone to find out where people went to when they died and I thought the church would be a good place to start. Surely with their connection to 'God' they would be in the know? So one Sunday morning, I dragged my dear friend Dee along, and we started to attend church.

Over the next six months I tried to recover from the battering blows life had been dealing me. I immediately started a course to learn a form of healing called 'Bowen' therapy, of which I qualified a year later. I also started feeling attracted to the vicar, so much so that I called him up one day and asked him out on a date. He said yes! He had been divorced for the past five years and I was now a widow. There were no rules to say we couldn't date. I thought I had fallen head over heels in love with the vicar. He needed rescuing, that's for sure and, I gave him my all to save him, or so I thought.

We talked about marriage, and suddenly, the conversations about marriage became inextricably linked to the vicar booking the church hall the Saturday of my fortieth birthday! I had in my mind that we would marry that day.

In February of 2003, a year after Stuart had died, the vicar and I went to Rome for a weekend. I had never visited Italy before and as Rome is believed to be one of the most romantic places on the planet, I was excited to be in such a wonderful city. The vicar had actually trained there for a while during his curacy. Each day we would go here and there visiting huge monumental churches and examining the culture. We ate al fresco in the evenings sitting under huge heaters while we drank in the Italian Roman atmosphere. I wanted to be ecstatically happy but there was just something that made me feel a little on edge. I ignored it though, after all here was I in the most romantic city in the world with a man I thought I was in love with. It was not until St Valentine's Day that the vicar decided to take me to see the famous Trevis Fountain, famed for throwing coins in and making wishes, a place where on Valentine's Day, romantic couples would go to confess their deepest love for each other and I'm sure many a proposal of marriage was carried out in front of this famously romantic landmark right in the centre of Rome. As we arrived, the vicar reached into his pocket,

"I've got something for you" He said.

"Oh my", I thought, "He's going to propose to me!" I felt a wave of fear and sickness. I suddenly wasn't sure about this. For a brief moment, a slight panic arose in me. It seemed too soon.

"Here's a coin; throw it in the fountain and make a wish" He said.

I'm not sure now if I was disappointed or relieved. I threw the coin in the fountain. I think I wished that I would return to Italy one day with my true love. In the meantime, I was glad that the vicar wasn't sure either. It felt like we were back on even footing. Neither of us knew what we wanted, but for now we were caught in the moment of two lost souls looking to be loved.

And so our relationship was played out like this. Sometimes he wanted me around; other times he made it clear he couldn't see me. I was confused and frustrated.

One night as we slept I had a very vivid dream. I was entering into a dark cave and inside was a dragon-like creature. I was terrified! I knew I had to enter inside and slay this dragon type serpent. I actually did it! I slayed him! But what made me wake up in a cold sweat was that in the dream I was on my own; the vicar was not with me.

I realise now that he didn't really love me and more to the point I didn't really love him. We were both broken people in a cycle of hurt and so lost we were clinging to each other for dear life! We returned home and our lives together limped along from day to day.

One day the vicar knocked on my door and as I opened the door I could tell by the look on his face that he was not bringing me good news.

Leading the way into the lounge I sat down next to him and leaned over to kiss him. The peck on the lips sent an unnerving feeling in my gut.

"What's the matter?" I asked,

He began to stutter and make contorted faces like he was writhing in pain.

"Just tell me what is wrong!?" I demanded.

Then came my old familiar enemy 'rejection'. His words scored deep into the already scarred tissue of my heart.

"Deb, I can't marry you, I don't love you."

"Why? Why are you saying this to me?"

"I've just been selfish and thinking about my own needs and when you came along with all your kindness I took advantage of you and I'm sorry. I think it's best if we stop seeing each other"

I really knew deep in my heart that we were not going to be together, but still I fought, I begged and pleaded.

He left. I didn't believe we wouldn't get back together. I would find a way.

Over the next few weeks, I felt bereft. My loss of Stuart and now the vicar; the wound cut deep. I was alone and I had no control over my life circumstances. No husband, no lover; no one to hold me, to talk to, to be with me; no one to give me an identity; as belonging to another. The pain and hurt seemed to be magnified more than I had ever experienced. This betrayal and rejection was too much for me to bear. I desperately wanted Stuart back in that moment, but I desperately wanted the vicar back too. What was wrong with me?

In that moment I needed to run away. I couldn't cope with my life; I was throwing in the towel!

By chance, in a magazine that discussed therapies and the work I had trained for, I saw an article for a spiritual holiday retreat in Murcia, Spain. It involved staying on a working finca, (a tomato plantation), and sleeping in a cave!

I sent an email for enquiry. The reply came:

Dear Debbie,

Thank you for your interest in our holiday retreat. At the moment there is only one cave complete, and if you're happy to accept this we will make a discount as you will be our first customer.

For a total cost of £200.00 you will receive full board and five complimentary treatments.

A few photographs were included which revealed a beautiful landscape of trees that looked to me like sanctuary.

I took up their kind offer and for the first time in my life, at the age of thirty nine, I flew off abroad and alone, to another country.

I was met at Murcia airport by one of the lady owners. As we drove for the hour long journey we chatted like we had been best friends all our lives and I felt very content. Before I knew it we had reached our destination, the beautiful working finca.

The place was breath taking. The plantation stretched out with row upon row of tomato plants all displaying their stunning, rouge beauty; colouring the landscape with a deep crimson glow. As I stood on the terrace in front of the caves, I could see the sparkle of the ocean in between the two far hills, the sun hitting the little rippled waves that made twinkling golden lights upon the surface of the water. The owner's house lay below the terrace on the opposite side of the make shift dirt track and nestled into the landscape the whole panoramic view was delightful.

There were two couples from England who had jointly purchased the land and the caves and together, with their children, they had created a wonderful, peaceful haven.

I was exhausted. I was broken and laden with self-help and spiritual books. I turned off my phone so as not to communicate with the world. I was an emotional and physical wreck and I needed to be there. As I looked out on this amazing view, my heart felt heavy as I had no one to share it with. Everyone, it seemed, had left my 'party' and to be honest, I wanted to leave it too!

The owners of the caves however were so kind and servant hearted, they could not do enough for me, and now leading me to my own little cave I was delighted to discover it had a front door which was within the newly built reception area. This area housed a communal dining area and off to the left bathroom and toilets. As I entered my cave, the heat of the day disappeared, only to be replaced with a cooler temperature; one of the assets of cave life is that air conditioning in summer or heaters in winter are not required as the temperature is always around 18 degrees centigrade. There was an actual lounge with seating and the most beautiful Spanish ornaments, leading through to a beautiful bedroom. All of this had been carved out of the stone of the hillside to make these amazing caves which were centuries old.

Over the week I would sleep peacefully in my little cave. In the morning I would emerge from the cave, shower and dress. My breakfast was placed in the reception area of the cave entrance. I ate fresh, colourful, wonderful food which had been prepared and made with love. The owners told me later on into the holiday that I had come like a wounded little bird; one they had wanted to nurture with love and care before they sent me on my way.

Years later, as I reflected on this vital part of my life, I could see the comparison with the man of God called Elijah in the Bible. 1 Kings 19, describes Elijah, battle weary and ready to die. He runs to the mountains to escape. He tells God he's had enough and he asks God to take his life. He lays down to sleep and twice an angel of the Lord wakes him up and commands him to eat and drink as the journey is too great for him. This was my Elijah time and just as Elijah went into the cave at Horeb to lodge there, I too, was hiding in my little cave in Spain!

After breakfast each day I would put on my huge sun hat and sit under the large olive tree just outside the entrance to the cave. In the peace and solitude I studied and read my books looking for the answers to the meaning of my life. At lunch time, one of the ladies would present me with an appetising salad with bread and meat, fresh fruit and a large jug of ice cold Sangria. After lunch I would read for an hour then enjoy a 'siesta' until 5 pm. I was so tired! I slept constantly. At 5pm each day one of the therapist's would come and deliver a treatment for me to enjoy; reflexology, aromatherapy massage, Hopi ear candles, Indian head massage and finally reiki. I felt uncomfortable with the reiki and I asked 'the god of the universe', whoever he was, to protect me from any bad spiritual influences. I say 'whoever he was' because after all of my study and practice of most eastern arts such as Feng Shui, crystal dowsing, and reiki, here I was now, broken, with no hope anymore. There was nothing real and tangible that I could look forward to and I wondered how I was going to be rescued from this pit. Nothing gave me a sense of peace, love or joy. Death, I realised, was inevitable for all of humanity and what was the point of living? I wasn't sure at all.

On the day of my final treatment, the therapist had left me to relax with the gentle music playing in the back ground. I lay on the couch, with the deepest feeling of hopelessness and I began to weep. Big, fat tears rolled down my cheeks and I lay still as they fell onto the couch towel below my face.

> *Exodus 2:23-25*
>
> *The Israelites groaned in their slavery and cried out, and their cry for help because of their slavery went up to God. God heard their groaning and He remembered His covenant (promise) with Abraham, with Isaac and with Jacob. So God looked on the Israelites and was concerned about them.*

Very quietly I looked up and spoke.

"God, if you really exist, please prove it to me, as right now, if there is nothing and you don't exist, there is no point in me staying on this planet."

I was at a point of complete surrender. A peace came over me.

Next day was Saturday 29th June, my birthday. I was forty! I had come for rest and recovery and by the time I left that place, I was ready for the next season of my life.

I left the retreat and, feeling rested and loved by these wonderful people, I flew back home. The first thing I did was visit the vicar. I wanted to show off my tan and how well I looked and I wanted to show him what he was missing.

"Wow you look amazing" he said.

My heart leapt and I thought "Yes! He still fancies me!"

But after a few weeks had gone by and, although I worked and lived as usual, I still had a deep sense of hopelessness in my heart. It was like I was walking through treacle. The vicar was not showing any interest at all and I was still feeling so depressed. It wasn't until a few years later I was told that the vicar had been given a warning to back off from me. Something he decided was the right thing to do and I am relieved he took this advice. I understand he is now remarried and very happy and I'm blessed by this too.

On the weekend of July 26th 2003, I decided to travel down to stay with my dear friend Dani. She had suffered a very bad car accident the previous year and although she was getting better she faced certain challenges due to her recent head injury. Dani lived in a little flat near Brighton. It was quiet and peaceful; a great place for her to recuperate. Near to the flat was an old Anglican church called St. Margaret's. We passed by it on the Saturday as we went for a gentle stroll in the summer sunshine. As I had been attending church, I asked Dani if we should go to church the next day. Dani's mum had died in the June of the previous year and Stuart had died in the February the same year. It was as if we needed to go to church to make some sense of their lives and their deaths. Dani had nearly died in the accident and so we felt we needed to go to church, but we didn't really understand why we needed to go. Dani's philosophy, as mine, was very much based on Eastern mysticism and, going into a church, an Anglican one at that, was quite controversial to us, but never the less we were going to go to church on a Sunday morning and it was our own decision!

That night we piled up a store of wine and cigarettes and chatted about the events of the past few years. It was emotional for both of us. We laughed, we cried and finally saying our goodnights we went to bed. As I lay down to sleep, my mind returned to Stuart and to the events of how I had now come to this point in my life.

CHAPTER 2

STUART -Perilous times

"This know also, that in the last days perilous times shall come.

For men shall be lovers of their own selves, covetous, boasters, proud, blasphemers, disobedient to parents, unthankful, unholy,

Without natural affection, trucebreakers, false accusers, incontinent, fierce, despisers of those that are good,

Traitors, heady, high minded, lovers of pleasures more than lovers of God[5] Having a form of godliness, but denying the power thereof: from such turn away.

For of this sort are they which creep into houses, and lead captive silly women laden with sins, led away with diver's lusts,

Ever learning, and never able to come to the knowledge of the truth" 2Tim:3

Having met my first husband at the grand old age of fifteen, married from the age of eighteen for fifteen years and, birthing two beautiful daughters Catherine and Jade, I had grown from girl to woman, or so I'd thought. I believe that not having had the early influence of a stable life from a daddy that loved me, I was now looking for that love in an older man. I wasn't interested at all in younger lads. My first husband was very street wise, and I lived a life of adventure. We were fairly well off, our children went to private school, and we holidayed in some of the most beautiful places in the world. I went shopping for clothes almost every day. My rings were diamonds and my watch was 22ct gold Constantin Vasheron. We partied at many places with a champagne lifestyle. Every year a car was ordered for Ascot and we spent the day with friends drinking and eating and gambling. I went to the gym most days and loved the lifestyle of how I was living. All seemed to be going well. As I reached my early thirties, I began however to feel as if I needed to do more with my life. I felt like I'd missed out on my younger years as well. It was then I decided to take a law course. I began to enjoy the experience of doing things for myself and realising I was quite clever. I was on a successful career path to becoming a solicitor, I was changing, and our marriage became more of a brother sister relationship. He was more involved with his work and I was getting more involved with mine. We never really spent quality time together as the years flew by. I was not content however to work in an office, and so made a huge leap of faith, and retrained to become a beauty therapist. This allowed me to enjoy a good income as I had converted a spare room into a beautiful salon. Suddenly making my own money and becoming independent, I became attracted to another man, when I reached the age of thirty four, myself and my husband divorced. I'm not proud to write about this and at the thought of sounding flippant, please forgive me, but out of respect for my children and my ex -husband I have decided not to reveal all of the details of our life together. Suffice to say, my life choices at the age of sixteen, were not that of a mature woman and not having had the right kind of guidance at that early stage of my life, led me to find love with an older man. Searching for love on a vast ocean, allowing the winds of life to take me, rather than being able to wisely navigate a clearly defined and carefully planned course led me to many experiences that would continually bring me back to the port of betrayal and rejection. Only on this occasion it was I who was the betrayer and rejecter.

The decree absolute arrived in the post mid-June of 1996 and my life was about to take me in a whole new direction. I was now running a very successful beauty and holistic therapy business from my home, and over the next ten years enjoyed a very good living from it. I had made a new friend called Dee through my beauty work, and another friend called Jess. We began to enjoy nights out and holidays together.

Dee, Jess and I decided to take a holiday in August that year to the beautiful island of Rhodes. We stayed in a beautiful place called Lindos. We spent most of the week partying all night and sleeping all day. It was great! For the first time in my life, I felt like I was answerable to no one; I was just me, nobody's wife, daughter, and mother; just me, and it felt liberating. As I look back, it was as though I was a teenager again and I felt as if I was getting a return of what I perceived to be my lost years. I was in my thirties, and as I returned from holiday, tanned, slimmed and feeling sexy, I realised I had started to feel really good about myself. I had a home, a great business and I was still young.

Still in the party mood on our return, we would go out into the nearby town as much as we could. One night we went out to a wine bar. The guy on the door gave me a wink. I was wearing my sexy Moschino black catsuit, which revealed my blonde hair and my tan. The doorman came into the wine bar at one point. He stood, overlooking the bar area, on a higher level. It made it easier for me and him to catch each other's eyes and smile across the crowded bar. The strange thing was, as

I dropped my gaze, I realised about five other men in my line of sight were smiling back at me too!

By the end of the night my doorman 'Stuart' had given me his card and I saw that by trade he was a wall and floor ceramic tiler. The next day as Dee and I were sitting in my lounge after dinner, I found myself holding his card in my hand. He was a very handsome man; strong and muscular and I was definitely attracted to him. As we giggled about how he had turned around as we left the wine bar, I knew I would see him again. I was acting like a love struck teenager.

Had I had been able to see into the future I would have ripped the card up and thrown it in the bin! However, I didn't. This man seemed exciting to me and I knew he desired me. The next day I telephoned Stuart; we chatted for hours and finally decided to meet up. The plan was I was going to pick him up from the wine bar and we would go out for drinks and a chat. I rocked up in my shiny new BMW, feeling fantastic in a short pleated black kilt type skirt and black sleeveless jumper. My hair was long, blonde and curly. I had done my nails and topped up my tan and smoothed my skin with coconut body oil; I was sizzling!

It wasn't long before Stuart moved in with me. He got on well with my girls. About two months after we moved in, he introduced us to his young daughter. She lived with her mum in a nearby town; apparently an old relationship that had gone wrong. The girls all got on well and we spent our days working and our nights partying. In a worldly way, life was pretty good.

One day after Stuart was taking his daughter home, my girls began to relay some of the things she had been telling them. She had told them that he was going to marry another woman just before he met me; a lady I'll refer to as Mary. It seemed Stuart had allowed Mary to gather a significant amount of debt and unfortunately, she lost her business. When he got home that evening I asked him about Mary. He told me that when he met her she was in a lot of debt and he supported her through it, but that they drifted apart and he had not seen her for months.

One thing I now reflect on and understand is that God promises us in His Word, that whatever is done in secret, will be shouted from the roof tops (Luke 12:3). It does seem that all through my life I've been pretty accurate when it comes to discerning when something is not quite right, or if I am given a revelation, even if I decide to ignore it, I still have that wisdom. This new revelation was a huge concern to me. I began to monitor Stuart's phone bill and sure enough there was one number that stood out. He had been on the phone for a couple of hours at a time. I began to cross check the times and dates and realised there were times when he was working at the stables, mucking out the horses for me for hours and other times were during the day when he was supposed to be working. Eventually I telephoned the number and Mary answered. She had no idea of my existence or even who I was and had no clue that Stuart and I were living together. She told me that on the day I had met him, (we swapped plenty of stories) he had taken her to get her wedding ring fitted and they were to be married. I was devastated! I couldn't believe this betrayal! It suddenly occurred to me that I had done exactly the same thing in my own marriage. I'd had an affair. It hadn't continued but was the catalyst to bringing my marriage to an end and I had betrayed and rejected many people in that process. Now, here I was, with the tables turned, experiencing once again the cold sting of betrayal and ultimate rejection.

Of course at this early stage, Stuart was able to convince me, that even though he had made plans to be married to Mary, when he met me, he knew he didn't really love Mary and was just going along with her decision to marry. When I asked him why he was calling her all the time, he said he felt guilty and wanted to make it up to her.

I demanded he leave the house, but in my weakness and with his smile and charming ways, I was beguiled and he would always work his way back into my heart. He was charming and I knew I loved him, or so I thought. The real truth was that this man was draining away my life in all areas and I couldn't seem to stop it. Over the next two years I had to sell my car as my debts escalated whilst I paid his debts! Slowly and surely my earnings were dwindling away and life wasn't so rosy.

Looking back now I reflect on the bible passage in 2 Timothy 3. It states this:

> "This know also, that in the last days perilous times shall come.
>
> 2 For men shall be lovers of their own selves, covetous, boasters, proud, blasphemers, disobedient to parents, unthankful, unholy,
>
> 3 Without natural affection, trucebreakers, false accusers, incontinent, fierce, despisers of those that are good,
>
> 4 Traitors, heady, high minded, lovers of pleasures more than lovers of God;
>
> 5 Having a form of godliness, but denying the power thereof: from such turn away.
>
> 6 For of this sort are they which creep into houses, and lead captive silly women laden with sins, led away with diver's lusts,
>
> 7 Ever learning, and never able to come to the knowledge of the truth"

This was happening to me, even the part about being incontinent. Stuart would often drink to access and wet the bed!

Stuart was jealous of my friends. I even stopped seeing Dee as he did not like her. I was like a puppet on a string and I was not in control. I took it as what some would call 'karma' for being unfaithful to my ex and hurting the girls and all the people who loved me. I lost it all, but that was not the end.

In late 1997, I began to realise I was emotionally drowning. I eventually absorbed the awful fact that I was allowing this man to damage my life and I told him he had to leave by the end of the year.

The girls were going on holiday with their dad and I thought it would be an ideal time to get him out while they were away. I knew Stuart would play up and I wanted to protect the girls from any unacceptable behaviour. The past two years had been a living hell and I wanted to extract Stuart from my life. Deep down, I knew it was the right thing to do.

I began the process of elimination in early November, advising him that he needed to find his own place and that it would be a good thing for him to spend time on his own, to learn about himself. I said he could spend Christmas with me and leave the day before the girls came back from their holiday with their dad. So the day before the girls were due back I had told Stuart it was his time to leave. He took most of his things, but he refused to let me go.

He would appear in the early evening on my doorstep. As I refused to open the door, he would sit on the lawn in front of my window calling my name. I would call his aunt or his brother for help and it was then that I discovered this was the way he handled situations when he was rejected. When his very first girlfriend had decided she couldn't carry on with their relationship, he parked his car on her drive and took the engine out so she could not move him on.

My good friend Jan who owned the livery where I kept my horses, had told me that she had discovered he had been sleeping in the train carriage which I used as a tack room. She liked Stuart, and seemed amused about his antics more than anything, but I knew she was concerned too.

One evening I called the local police. Stuart's behaviour was becoming more erratic and this time as he rocked to and fro on the lawn he cried out,

"Debs, I love you please, please, please, let me in"

The police said they would take him away. At that time the anti-stalking law was not legally in place and I knew that many women had been murdered by ex-spouses and partners because none of their complaints to the police had been taken seriously.

And so that very evening, due to the police not having this legal instrument to effect an arrest, they dropped him approximately ten minutes away from my house, at a local public house. That night my dog Teddy barked several times and I began to feel frightened. The next morning I went to let the dog out in the back garden and Stuart came rushing in and grabbed me. I screamed in absolute fright!

"Sssshhh!" He said, putting his fingers to my lips. My heart was beating fast.

I could easily read his face. He was just delighted he was holding me and kept kissing me and telling me he loved me and he would never hurt me. He held me tightly as we stood by the garage door.

Common sense kicked in and I said,

"You are freezing, come into the kitchen and I'll make you some tea and toast"

I tried to stay calm, knowing all the external doors to the street were locked and I would not have time to fight him and escape.

"Oh, thanks Debs, can I just use the toilet?"

"Yes" I said and, as he went into the downstairs toilet, I immediately picked up the phone and dialled the police. I told them what had just

happened and they said they would come straight away. By this time I had unlocked the front door and opened it wide. If Stuart wasn't going to leave, then I was. As he came out of the toilet, I realised he had heard my conversation and he was furious! He stormed past me,

"You f'ing bitch" he said as he shot out of the house.

The police arrived a few moments later or should I say an [1]Alf Ventris look-alike appeared at the door.

"We can't do anything I'm afraid." He said, "He's committed no crime, it's just a 'domestic' in our eyes, if you want to stop him coming here you'll need a court order."

The policeman looked as if he wasn't bothered and I felt he saw me as a stupid woman, getting hysterical about an argument with this man.

"Is there nothing you can do? This man is acting really strangely; I've never seen him like this before" I pleaded.

"Look, I'll go and see if I can find him and have a word" he said trying to placate my anger.

I told him he had been sleeping up in the nearby tack room so off he went in search of Stuart.

In the meantime I got hold of a solicitor. I dressed and went for the emergency appointment. He gave me a letter and instructed me to give it to Stuart. If he did not adhere to the letter we could go to court for an injunction.

"Give him the letter". I thought this was not likely. I was too afraid at this point. Driving home I began to realise that this situation was really affecting my free will, and as well as feeling frightened, I was also annoyed to say the least.

As I pulled up onto the drive, I had caught a glimpse of Stuart

---

[1] Alf Ventris was a character in a 1960's UK police series and portrayed an old policeman who did as little as possible in his job at the police station and was just biding his time till he retired!

staggering toward the house. My heart was thumping inside the cavity of my chest and I could feel the blood pounding in my head. Gripped with fear I tried to reverse the car out but I was too late and suddenly, he was there opening the car door.

I tried to stay calm and asked him what he was doing. I told him the police were looking for him; that he needed to go before they arrived. He laughed in my face and I caught a strong waft of alcohol from his breath. I grabbed my mobile phone as I got out of the car. I knew I needed to run, quickly. He grabbed my mobile phone and threw it up in the air as if casting away an old piece of rubbish. As it landed onto the concrete, I noticed the back battery panel came off and the battery was now lying away from the main body of the phone. I tried to come across as annoyed, yet inside I watched myself, heart beating rapidly. I could not believe this was all happening! Here I was, wrestling with a man I had shared two years of my life with; the man I once loved and cared for; the man whom I still loved, yet had to reject as I did not have the ability to accept and work through with him, the choices of how he lived his life. His eyes looked vacant, he looked like a stranger to me,

"Let's go in for a coffee?" he said, panting hard and licking and wetting the bottom lip with the tip of his tongue. A quick internal reference to my survival at this point came back as a big fat 'No!' to this request. He was acting so strangely and although I knew he was drunk, it felt that even that was not the reason he was behaving with an almost sinister air about him.

"No, I'm not letting you in the house Stuart, just go and leave me alone" I cried out!

Suddenly freeing myself from his hold, I picked up the phone and the battery. He grabbed me and held me down on the bonnet of the car. This was it! He was going to kill me! I knew my rejection of him was not what he wanted to hear, but I was stuck between a rock and a hard place. If I let him inside the house to talk, I would probably not come out alive. If I decided not to raise his hopes, I still had to fight him off.

I realised that the six foot high laurel hedge that surrounded the gently sloping driveway leading to my front door was not helpful at all to me in this current situation, as it was doing its job too well of providing the privacy from the roadside that I was normally grateful for. In my mind, I realised there was no one to help. As we grappled; me to get free and him to overpower, I caught sight of the little girl from next door looking out the upstairs window. Would she get help? Does she know I'm in danger? Questions and answers rolling around in my mind as I fought for my life! It was as if I was there, but I wasn't there; a surreal atmosphere of danger; another part of me looking on like a trainer in a boxing ring, whispering instructions and almost offering an insight to myself, with this terrifying situation in hand.

I suddenly cried out,

"God, please help me."

In an instant Stuart let go of me and staggered toward the porch doors. I ran to my neighbour's house. Hopefully, the little girl would have told an adult I was in trouble? I knocked frantically on the door but nobody came. My heart was beating fast and with one look behind me I saw that I was still on my own. With my hands trembling, I tried to 'stick' together the battery with the phone but couldn't remember how to do it. I had to run away from this place; it was too near my attacker. No one was going to open this door. I was in shock and with my mind racing, I ran across the main road trying to make distance between myself and the perpetrator. Suddenly there was an almighty sound of crashing and breaking of glass coming from the direction of my house. Not daring to look back, I ran down the road where an elderly couple was putting shopping into the house from their car. Screaming in panic and shaking violently I cried out,

"Help me, please help me!"

The man and his wife brought me into their house and tried to calm me.

"Please call the police," I cried *"He's going to kill me!!"*

It was as if they couldn't understand me. The man said he would go up to my house and speak to Stuart.

"No! Don't go there, please he will kill you too, please call the police!"

On reflection, I remember they didn't say too many words and I think they may have thought I was some crazy woman. It is only as I write this now that I realise I never went back to thank them for helping me that day.

The man called the police. He was told that there had already been an emergency call made and the police were on their way.

"Maybe the neighbour did call the police after all?" I thought.

I could not stay and wait. I left and stood outside the neighbour's house. It was as I drew nearer that I could detect a slight, wailing siren. I moved closer to the house; my new found bravery came, knowing the police were on their way. Keeping a discreet distance I saw black smoke billowing out of a side vent from the bedroom wall. The wailing sounds were from the smoke alarms in my house.

"Oh no! He's setting fire to my house! He's going to kill himself in my house!" Panic set in, *"Oh no, my dog is in the garage; he will die too"*. I couldn't breathe! I was in a horror story and I was unable to step away from it!

A small police car pulled up with one man inside! One man! And it was the Alf Ventris lookalike!

"Is that it?" I thought, *"One man to save me and fight off this mad man!?"*

The police man looked at me.

"Has he got a gun?"

"I'm not sure, I don't think so," I said, unconvincingly, and as my thoughts were starting to race, I thought to myself,

"Oh no, he may have a gun, I'd never thought about that, he is acting so violently."

The policeman broke my thoughts. Looking back it was obvious he wasn't going to risk being shot at, not so near retirement, and without a thought for my safety it seemed, the policeman then went on to say,

"You'll have to move your car out of the drive."

Move my car? Was he mad?

"I'm not going down there!" I said, pointing to the car sitting on the drive.

As I looked down the drive, I could see Stuart's silhouette standing in the hall way. Although the front door was locked, he was standing and peering through the middle panel which used to be glazed, but was now glass free. The thick black smoke covering his face as it billowed out through the door panel;

"I can't go near him he'll kill me!" I cried out.

"You will need to move the car" the policeman said, in a stern voice. Looking back I would have told him to drive it off himself, but obediently, I quickly ran to the car door and jumped into the car! My hands and legs were shaking so much as I grappled with the keys to put into the ignition. I locked the doors and started the engine. I couldn't look at the front door as I reversed onto the street and parked up. Just at that moment what looked like the flying squad arrived, followed by two fire engines. A brief momentary waft of shame came over me as I thought,

"What will the neighbours think?"

As I looked down the road I saw my wonderful friend Jan coming towards me with her sister. I gladly ran into her arms! I needed a friend right then and here she was.

"How did you know this was all happening?" I asked as we hugged.

"I was worried about you and telephoned you. Stuart answered, and

I could hear your smoke alarms going off, I asked him where you were and he just said that you were safe. That worried me so I called the police."

Jan had discovered that Stuart had been living in the horse carriage we had for my horses which we kept in livery on her property. She had told me that she had discovered a hangman's noose set up in there, along with empty bottles of vodka and tablets.

This is it, I realised. He wants to die. I was reminded of the times he would say that I had not seen his final 'Coups de Gras', a title he took from a song by his favourite band The Stranglers. He also told me that he would be like a 'Phoenix' rising from the ashes.

At that moment an ambulance arrived and I waited for the body bag to be brought out. His final Coups de Gras!

All of a sudden a shout came from one of the police officers,

"He's out, he's out, he's out!" he shouted!

The police scattered in all directions, some battering down the front door so that the firemen could start putting out the fire, while others ran down nearby walkways onto the fields that backed onto my property.

Stuart was caught escaping over the fields and like a scene from a movie he was cuffed and arrested. As he walked past me, with tears streaming down his face he shouted across to me,

"I'm still here Debs!"

That evening after the fire, my ex-husband was kind enough to let me stay at his home with our girls. They were very upset and we all wanted to be together. I was so traumatised by the whole drama that when I woke the next morning I had wet the bed.

In late January 1999, Stuart was sentenced to four years in prison for arson with intent to endanger lives. Not my life, but that of the fire officers who were trying to put the fires out as he kept lighting more fires. He threatened them not to come into the house.

As this was classed as malicious damage, the insurance company covered the refurbishing of the house as well as replacing our lost possessions and paying for the rent on a rented property which miraculously came up for rent the day after the fire. It was furnished and suited us perfectly.

The aftermath of the fire was a hard time. I took the girls to Tenerife at the end of February for a short holiday and even though it was good to get some winter sunshine I was bereft. I felt lonely and depressed and I began to have panic attacks.

I decided I would try meditation to help calm me. I would spend an hour or so with my legs crossed, (I couldn't quite manage the Lotus position!) breathing in the golden light and breathing out the blackness that was from within. I did feel calm as the breathing techniques had been given to me by a self-help group I had been referred to because of my panic attacks.

I threw myself into the project of the refurb of the house, as it was quite a difficult task choosing décor and furniture for a whole house that had been set on fire. Fortunately the roof had not been affected so it was more of a redecoration job.

Life became peaceful. The girls however, spent more time with their dad. They too had battle scars and were frightened even more by the dark and did not like the house we had rented. I sensed something strange in the girl's room but I decided it was due to all the drama we had all been through. However one night as I tried to sleep, a heavy weight just rested on my body. My heart began to beat faster. I had been studying many holistic practices, and I spoke out in a clear voice,

"Are you of the light?"

Immediately the heaviness went.

In my quest to find the peace I longed for, I reached out even more into the field of Eastern Mysticism. I began to attend workshops on the worship of angels and also I began to study the I Ching; an Eastern teaching of the study of energy in our lives; Yin and Yang; light and dark. I also attended workshops on crystal dowsing and chakra energy unblocking. As I moved back into my home I began to organise healing workshops and used crystal dowsing to tell people what their body needed for healing. I'd kept my previous home telephone number, as my business, although temporarily affected by the fire, was able to continue, and to be honest, I lived off the increase in the local clientele who all wanted to hear my story. The fire had made front page news as well as the small village being entrenched with the gossip of my demise. I had a friend who helped me through all of this time called Brenda. She was a clairvoyant and was always on hand to give me free readings and 'helped me to direct my path in life'. Looking back now, I have my reservations about this friendship.

One day the phone rang and I answered. As the voice spoke my heart began to beat fast,

"Debs, it's me. Please don't put the phone down" It was Stuart, speaking softly.

"I won't put the phone down" I said and I began to weep as Stuart attempted to unfold all that he wanted to say,

"Debs, I'm so sorry for how things turned out. I was so stupid; I realise that now. Look I've been meditating and getting into this way of living by love. I've even joined the prison Ashram; I have a Buddhist monk come to visit me and he has been teaching me how to live life on another higher level of being."

"I've been meditating too" I said. I told him about the courses I was doing and the work I had been doing in my business. I called myself a 'light worker.'

As we chatted over the next few weeks I began to feel that Stuart had changed. His words and actions seemed so different. I felt the love that I had originally held for him begin to glow again.

I confided in my friend. I'll refer to her as Miriam. She was another clairvoyant and I had many readings from her too, always giving me guidance as to how I should proceed and telling me of warnings and of blessings. When she heard I'd been speaking to Stuart and that I was contemplating going to visit him, she was delighted and said she thought we should always be together. She would see it in the Tarot cards and so she offered to drive me to the prison out in Rutland. Miriam never came in to the visit but she would wait for two hours, the length of the prison visiting hours, outside in the car.

When I walked into the visiting room, Stuart looked different. He was slim and looked very well; his blue eyes were glistening and we sat opposite each other just chatting. His smile was as broad as ever and his charm once again melted my heart. Something was different this time though. He was living a disciplined life. Easy, I know, while in prison and away from the world, but he looked like he had gained some inner strength and he no longer seemed needy or vulnerable.

Before long I was visiting every two weeks. Strangely though and without realising it, I began to get sick. I was falling into a deep depression. In fact it got so bad I could no longer work. I kept up my most loyal customers, but each day, if I was not going to visit Stuart, I would just sleep. One day my youngest daughter came back from school and I was still asleep from when she had left me that morning. I thank God for her now as she stayed with me in those days as much as she could; she was worried for me.

My credit card debt was building up, with my lack of work and petrol costs with driving to and from the prison. I was also sending lump sums of money to odd addresses given to me by Stuart so that he could acquire phone cards. I would then spend the majority of my time talking to him when I wasn't visiting him. Towards the middle of the second year of his sentence he was relocated to an 'open' prison and we were able to utilise visitation rights visit every fortnight. Plus, Stuart could leave the prison grounds all of the Saturday and Sunday having to return just for the evenings to his cell. I booked a hotel near the prison where we spent the two days eating out. Sometimes, he only had one day, so I would collect him in the morning at eight o'clock and he would then drive us back to my home and we would spend the day together, returning to the prison for seven o' clock in the evening. Overall, we covered nearly four hundred and fifty miles each Sunday. The cost of that alone was coming off my credit cards, paying one off with the money from another one. I realise now, that I had somehow become obsessed with this relationship. In fact, sadly, I lived for the day that Stuart was going to come home. In the year 2000 we decided that we would get married on one of the weekends that we had a Saturday and a Sunday free. I bought a beautiful pink dress with a matching dusty pink cardigan and silver shoes. I was only eight stone and I felt my figure was perfect in this dress. It was not a wedding type dress. We were to be married at Sleaford registry office, which turned out to be a wooden hut! I bought Stuart a new suit and bought the wedding rings; all courtesy of my credit cards.

We married on 20th September 2000 and our witnesses were a couple of girls from the flower factory Stuart had been working at, while residing at Her Majesty's Prison.

During the times of communicating with Stuart, I felt compelled to write to him every day and he would telephone me about two or three times a day. He even got someone to smuggle in a mobile phone which he hid at work so he could call me. These calls became all-consuming and began to rule my life. If friend's came around and I was on the phone to Stuart, I was too afraid to let him know that I had company. He would keep me talking for hours and my friends would just leave. My whole life revolved around him.

By January 2001, Stuart was home, on parole. If he remained crime free in this probation period, he would stay free.

So, our married life began. Due to my attempts to try to be happy, I got into a deeper depression and started to take anti-depressant tablets. I became numb to my life and ended up being swept along and not really caring what I needed to do.

My clairvoyant friend would continually do 'free' readings for me and I would wait in hope for what she promised the cards were revealing. Travel, happiness and all the trappings of how that would become possible.

Looking back at this time, I am utterly surprised at my behaviour and I firmly believe I was under some sort of enchantment; a sort of spell, or curse. It's almost as though I'm not writing about myself!

In June 2001, a friend of mine called Bruce opened a restaurant and I went to the opening party. It was obvious the waiters were not coping with the volume of people, so I helped out with clearing plates and serving the buffet. I attended the party on my own as Stuart said he had to work. I had lost all my confidence and rarely went out of the house, but the invite felt safe as it was all my family attending the party. It felt good to be with other people and get away from my life with Stuart. It wasn't long before Bruce asked me to work for him, and I agreed. I was able to build up my confidence, and even took over as manager of the restaurant. As I worked, my confidence built up. I stopped taking the anti-depressants and began to feel alive for the first time in years.

One day in late July, Stuart told me he was unhappy with his life with me and wanted to move out. I wasn't really shocked. We had been drifting along and I felt he was drifting away from me. He decided he would leave. It wasn't long before I discovered by the evidence of his telephone bills that he was calling a number pretty regularly and was talking for up to two hours. I called the number and his old girlfriend answered. Another stab of rejection and hurt. As soon as Stuart knew I'd found out about his girlfriend, he wanted to come back home; he said he was sorry. He did not come back to live with me for quite a while, but at the beginning of December 2001 he turned up one particular day, with boxes full of ceramic floor tiles and asked me if he could tile my lounge floor. One thing he was good at was tiling. He had been trained by an Italian firm and he could tile anything. The floor looked fabulous and him seeing I was thrilled, he offered to buy the Christmas tree, and so we went into town and Stuart bought the most amazing huge tree. The house was looking cosy and lovely and I began to believe that maybe he was now ready to settle down and become a proper husband to me. We went out on dates and we bought presents for all the family.

On Christmas Eve, we took my girls to a restaurant for a lovely meal. My youngest daughter was staying with us but as we settled down for the festivities, I began to feel unease. Stuart's phone had been quiet and usually he had frequent calls. After watching television for a while Stuart said he was going for a bath. I waited a while and went up to the bathroom. He was in the bath with his phone in hand and leaning over him I took the phone and read his message,

"I wish I was in the bath with you," were the words from the text message. As I stood outside the bathroom door, I looked into my daughter's bedroom. She was happily reading a book. I looked at the message once more as a piercing dagger of rejection, hurt and betrayal plunged the depths of my heart. Doubled up in my painful emotion, I sobbed and my daughter came out of her room.

"What's wrong mum?" she said. I began to tell her that Stuart was still seeing his ex -girlfriend and I'd had enough. She was upset but said,

"Mum, just tell him to go"

He had been drinking and I knew he wasn't sober enough to drive so I told him he had to leave in the morning. I slept with my daughter and at six o'clock in the morning I was standing over the bed waking Stuart up.

"You need to go right now" I said.

He got dressed and came and joined me in the kitchen. As he stood against the drawer unit, I recall saying to him as I looked him straight in the eyes,

"You do the devil's work, you do!"

"No I don't!" he said, but with a look of alarm on his face.

"Oh yes you do" I said, *"and I'm not standing for it anymore! Leave now and don't ever come back here again"* and this time, I knew I truly meant it.

My best friend Dee rescued us and invited us to her home for Christmas Day. I did, however spend the majority of those Christmas holidays on my own, just watching films and getting lost in stories rather than look at my own, very painful story.

To really push me further into an abyss of heartbreak and fear, Bruce decided to fire me when we had argued about his aggressive behaviour toward me. He attempted to reinstate me a week later, but I was finished with bullies. I must have turned a corner, I thought. I called my friend Miriam for a tarot card reading, but even she was suddenly very aggressive toward me, saying she never wanted to see me, or Stuart, ever again! Her voice actually sounded like a rasping demon on the telephone,

"I never want to see any of you ever again" she rasped. This was from a lady who was normally soft and gentle in her manner. I honestly didn't know why she said this! It was only years later, when I became a Christian, that I realised that the Spirit within me was one that the spirit within her had recognised! I was reading the following passage, when all of a sudden it dawned on me that this woman had influenced my life massively in regard to me pursuing my relationship with Stuart. I cast my mind back to the day when she had driven me to that first prison visit to see Stuart after the fire; the times the readings were all about us being together. The way I felt almost being buffeted along

on life's waves not really having any clear direction. Through naming the demon that I believe Stuart was living by, I truly believe I broke a strong influence of oppression, control and fear over my life.

It reads this in Acts:

> Acts 16-18 *One day, on our way to the place of prayer, a slave girl ran into us. She was a psychic and, with her fortune telling, made a lot of money for the people who owned her. She started following Paul around, calling everyone's attention to us by yelling out, "These men are working for the Most High God. They're laying out the road of salvation for you!" She did this for a number of days until Paul, finally fed up with her, turned and commanded the spirit that possessed her, "Out! In the name of Jesus Christ, get out of her!" And it was gone, just like that"*

And just like that, I felt the control and rule that Stuart had over my life was gone! I felt free; however, convincing him that I no longer wanted him in my life was another story.

The old behaviour arose and Stuart began to pester me. He would come to the house, crying and begging me to take him back and when he began to realise that I was serious and he had received a letter from my solicitor regarding a divorce, he became worse. I would come home to find wires pulled out of the external wall as he tried to destroy my things. Stupidly, I had taken a car loan out for him and he was still driving the car and not paying the instalments. I'd had enough and called the police. Rather than the airy fairy police officer I had experienced from my past drama with Stuart, the policeman that came round was an inspector. He took time to listen to my story and he explained that the law had changed recently and there was now an anti-stalking law that he believed Stuart had broken. This man went into action and within two days Stuart was arrested and charged. On his way out of the police station he was served with a warrant from the courts to prohibit him from coming near the house. He was also told very sternly by the inspector to return my car to me or they would charge him with theft. He returned the car to my friends home and together with his girlfriend, sprayed her perfume inside the car, as if to say,

"Stuart's mine now!"

I believe the perfume was called 'Angel' which was very appropriate, as I felt she had taken my place and I was very glad of that!

I began to try to pick myself up and get on with my life. As I no longer worked at the restaurant, I needed to get an income quickly.

A few days before the end of January 2002, I attended a psychic event, mainly to work at giving reflexology treatments to earn some money. I'd made arrangements that day for my youngest daughter to go back to her dad's after school and stay there overnight, as I knew I would be out until around 10pm. As I waited for the evening sessions to begin at the psychic event, I noted the hall full of psychics. One of them was a strange looking man who said he was a wizard, he asked me if I'd like a free reading. I took up his offer and he began to tell me about a tree and that he could see someone hanging from it. He was so weird, around the age of eighty, who then proceeded to ask me out on a date! I, of course, declined. By 7pm, the event was in full flow; groups of women all desperate to see if they were going to meet a tall, dark stranger who would whisk them off their feet, waited in long queues for their turn. My stall was empty! Nobody wanted a foot treatment. I decided I'd had enough. I packed up my things and left. Psychic events weren't for me.

I drove straight to Dee's. I needed my friend's love and care and a bottle of red wine! Two hours later, I was on my way home to bed. Pulling onto the driveway, I turned off the ignition, got out of the car, locked it and put my key in the porch door. Once inside, I had literally just opened the front door when someone grabbed me from behind. I looked and saw Stuart. He was wearing a huge puffa jacket and stuffed inside I saw a large rope folded up. He was holding a crow bar in his hand which was raised up above my head.

He was breathing heavily,

"Get inside the house Debs, just get inside the house" he said very calmly.

At this point, had I not just shared a bottle of wine with my friend, I know I would have tried to fight him and I honestly believe he would have killed me there and then. As it was, I felt a little relaxed and my instinct kicked in,

"Oh Stuart! What are you doing?" I said, *"You nearly gave me heart attack"*

I continued and kissed him, *"Oh I've missed you baby,"* as I began to cry; I was crying because I was frightened but he thought I was crying because I'd missed him.

"Where have you been?" he asked urgently, *"I've been waiting all day for you!"*

I told him about the event and how I never made any money and he seemed to calm down and he placed the crow bar on the kitchen counter.

"If you'd have come back with a man, he would have got this" he said, pointing at the crow bar angrily.

I made us coffee and put the dog out in the garage. I don't know why I did that but I just felt he needed to be out of the way. I also felt strongly that I wasn't safe. I looked up at the metal steel girder supporting the roof and had a brief vision of a rope hanging from it. I shuddered and shut the garage door.

We sat in the lounge drinking coffee. I was visibly shaking but didn't even want to put the fire on because I had visions of Stuart pushing me into the fire. I was so very frightened.

He began to tell me he was going to live in China at a Buddhist temple but then he would change his tale and say he was going to open a ceramic tile shop in Redditch! His thoughts seemed to be all over the place.

At one point he kept asking me if I'd met anyone else, even though I had absolutely no intention of meeting anyone else right now! I became aware of that same sinister look in his eyes. He would be looking down at his feet and close one eye as if lining up a rifle to fire a shot. At the same time, he used his tongue to push out one side of his cheek as if he was planning his next move. Because of this, a fear arose in me and I felt I needed to act fast. I knew he was thinking I'd lied and I had been out with another man today and I also knew he wanted to make sure no other man would ever have me again.

I tried to divert his mind and I said I would make another coffee. It was then he told me he had hired a car and he needed to bring it off the road, in case the police came by, as my address was on their alert list. Looking me directly in the eye, he said,

"Don't go calling the police will you?"

"Don't be silly, baby" I said, *"I'm not calling anyone"* and I didn't. I was so afraid he would come back and catch me on the phone, then kill me and himself, before the police arrived. I watched and saw to my horror, he had hired a people carrier with blacked out windows. I had visions of him carrying my body away in the back seat.

When he arrived back inside the house, I led the way back into the lounge, I wanted to stay talking, keeping him engaged with silly conversation, pretending to be 'normal' with him, with us, as if this had all never happened, yet all the time my body trembled. I told him I was cold I didn't want him to know I was trembling with fear. As the night wore on other expectations were brought into the mix. I will leave that there but hence to say it was a long night.

As dawn began to break, I began to wonder how this was going to play out. He was satisfied enough to think that we still had a future together, and I was not going to say anything different at this point in time. I just wanted him to leave. Finally I plucked up the courage and said,

"Stuart, you'll need to go soon, the girls will be coming by to get their sports kits for school. I don't want them to see you as they will call the police"

This was a lie of course, but Stuart seemed to accept this. I watched him and became unsettled when I realised this reality of him having to go brought him back to the reality of just where we were in the midst of a developing drama. I watched as his eyes darted from side to side, I imagined his mind desperately searching for words that would allow him to get back control of me. As I watched him I knew he was still sensing this. It was then that he came up with an idea.

"Let's meet up tonight?" he said, *"I've got something I want to show you"*

"Ok that sounds exciting" I replied, but deep inside my gut was that whatever it was it was, it was not going to be good for me. I agreed to meet him, mustering the enthusiasm to allow him to believe everything now was going to be alright between us.

At 7.30 am, on Thursday 31st January 2002, Stuart waved goodbye to me with his big smile. He shouted over from the car,

"See you later, Debs" and then he drove off in his hired 'people carrier' with blacked-out windows. And I never saw him again.

I was left with the memories of the night before, feeling almost numb I locked the front door and going back into the kitchen I noticed he'd left the crow bar and the rope on the floor, it was time to call the police.

The constable that answered my call provided me with his theory to my problem.

"Well, if you let him in what do you expect?"

Because of his remark, I felt that I was to blame and felt ashamed to say anymore. I asked when the police officer dealing with the case was next on duty and he told me it was at 6pm. I immediately got dressed and went to my friends where I kept my horse. I showed her the rope and crow bar and she said they belonged to her. She'd been out for most of the previous day and we both realised that Stuart had been milling around and took the items which were now on the back seat of my car. I made sure I was not on my own and I went to see my friend Dee. She was so angry with how the police had treated my urgent call that she got straight onto the police. Within twenty minutes the police man dealing with the case was at her door with a lovely woman officer.

When this policewoman came in, I felt a huge flood of relief. She oversaw the interview and as we were talking somebody knocked on the front door. I began to shake and cry,

"It's him" I whispered.

The policewoman got hold of a heavy object and said *"Don't worry. Open the door. I'm right behind you"*

I couldn't risk it! He could grab me and take me as a hostage. I was too scared. She opened the door, this brave little lady and a sigh of relief was given when we saw that it was another police officer at the door.

The police woman, named Judy, knew that Stuart had arranged to meet me that evening so she asked me to call him and arrange a meeting. I was too afraid even to speak to him so eventually she decided to call him and asked him to give himself up.

He said there was no way he was giving himself up. He told Judy to tell me he would be a like a 'Phoenix rising from the ashes'. Judy asked me if I knew what that meant and I told her he always said he would overcome anything. I also told her he always spoke of his 'Coup de Gras', a final denouement of his life.

Judy decided for our safety to move Dee and I to a hotel in

Birmingham that night, as she felt this was a dangerous time for me. She asked me where we could go with the children; somewhere Stuart would not think of. The place chosen was with Dee's friend Jess, who lived in Bristol.

The next day I and my two daughters left for our 'safe house', fleeing from the arms of a man who I was married to and who wanted to take my life. It was so unreal.

Every day over the following week, Judy would contact me and tell me what Stuart had been up to in his evasion from the police. He had never took the car back to the hire place and now his charge would also include stealing a car. I knew he didn't care anymore about what the outcome would be, he had lost control over me and he didn't know where I was, this was a dangerous time. By now Judy had taken my mobile phone, Stuart had left messages to indicate threatening behaviour toward me with a mixture of an unquenchable love he had for me. This was to be used as further evidence in the future.

On February 8th, we had planned a holiday with friends to Lanzarote for a family holiday. Stuart was initially joining us as we had booked it in late October of the previous year. I had taken his details off the booking form when he left the home back in December. He knew this, yet presumed we would still be going. The date of the flight was February 8th 2002, at 11.30am from our local airport.

Judy called me at Jess's house.

"What will he do now Debs?" She asked. *"Everything else you said he would do, he has done!"*

"I think today is the most dangerous day Judy," I said. *"He will quite possibly come to the airport, I'm worried what his final Coup de gras will be.*

Judy had already explained from the very start that it was not wise for us to go to Lanzarote as we would have no protection. To be honest a holiday was the last thing on my mind! I also was taking no chances!

She told me the airport was on full alert and that police were all ready for anything that might happen. On the Friday morning I spoke to Judy first thing. She told me she had spoken to Stuart's 'current girlfriend' who had explained to her that he had left her home that morning and told her he was handing himself in to the police. I told Judy he wouldn't do that; I knew he was not in the right state of mind.

We waited patiently at Jess's house and at midday I called Judy.

"Have you heard anything?" I asked.

There was a pause over the phone then Judy spoke,

"Deb, I was going to come down and tell you; I didn't want to tell you over the phone"

"Tell me Judy, what's happened?"

"Stuart's killed himself Deb. He hung himself"

It was as if a surge of electricity ran through my body.

Stuart was dead.

I was shocked.

Judy proceeded to tell me the details.

"He had made a hang man's noose and hung himself from a tree at the lakes, a place we used to walk the dogs. His body was discovered by a passer-by who called the police."

Stuart had left a suicide note in his pocket but Judy told me not to read it as it was not a very nice letter and I didn't need to see the contents. I never did, I trusted her word.

The effects of Stuart's death were far reaching and my regret was the pain it had caused for my daughters; the repercussions of which, were felt years later, the consequences playing out in the future lives of both my children.

I had been desperately looking for love and attracted someone who was just as desperate and so broken he could not have given me the love that he also did not have.

I didn't attend Stuart's funeral. The funeral director said my flowers were torn from the coffin and stamped on by Stuart's family. His ashes were taken by his daughter of which I was glad about; they meant more to her than to me.

• •

THE NEW STORY- 2003

CHAPTER 3

Awakening

> *There is no fear in love; but perfect love casts out fear, because fear involves punishment, and the one who fears in not perfected in love.*
>
> *1 John 4:18*

Now, here I was over a year later, getting ready to go to church in a small sleepy village in the south of England. I was broken, looking for answers and wondering how I allowed myself to get to this point in my life.

I finally drifted off to sleep. My sleep was troubled that night and on waking I felt the heaviness on my heart, the cost of dwelling on the past few years of my life.

My friend Dani and I arrived at the village church which was St Margaret's and duly seated ourselves in a pew. We were given what was called an 'Order of Service' which basically described what was going to happen during the service- when and what songs would be sung, along with the words. This was extremely helpful. I read the front page. There was a baptism of a little girl whom we had never met. As I glanced over at her and her family I could see that the little girl had Down's syndrome. She was going to be baptised in the service. I skimmed through the songs and noticed that they were all pertinent to me in some way.

The first song was 'Be still for the presence of the Lord'. Our home church sang this song and it resonated with me in that I began to feel a presence of such love and peace when it was sung softly, tears would flow.

The next song was 'I, The Lord of sea and sky'. The words begin;

I, The Lord of sea and sky, I have heard my people cry, all who dwell in dark and sin my hand will save.

I, who made the stars of night, I will make their darkness bright,

Who will bear my light to them? Whom shall I send?

Here I am Lord, is it I Lord?

I have heard you calling in the night, I will go Lord if you lead me, and I will hold your people in my heart.

It was as this song began that I started to weep, tears began to trickle down my face, first softly and then my body racked with deeper sobs. They were uncontrollable. Then suddenly there was a voice through this singing. Not an audible voice but a real a knowing of being spoken to:

"Debra, Debra, I know what are you are going through and from now on I am going to take care of you"

In that instant I knew it was God speaking to me. I sobbed and sobbed even more. I didn't care who was listening or if I looked foolish in this little Anglican church in the midst of a sleepy village. I had been on a long journey which had been fraught with danger and death and now I was falling into the arms of my real Father, my Daddy.

Over the past month since I had asked God to reveal Himself to me. I had been waking very early every morning at exactly 3.33am and would stay awake for about two hours. (In Jeremiah 33:3 it says "Call to Me and I will answer you, and I will tell you great and mighty things that you do not know.") I had been having strange dreams of being called and now the words I'd heard in church were penetrating all of my being. I'd never experienced the tangible love of a real Daddy on earth.

I cast my mind back to the man I thought was my father when I was young. He was never demonstrable with his love and affection to me; he often got drunk and my memory is of a man who was like a stranger to me, cold and unloving.

The man I was brought up to believe was my father died of cancer when I was seven years old. I was taken to the mass the evening before the funeral and was upset because my mummy was crying. I never really understood about the fact that I would never see this man again.

Mum went on to marry a lovely man, my step father Jack, who was a wonderful father to us. He looked after us and in my older years I certainly knew what a kind hearted servant hearted man he was.

A few years later God revealed to me another man who was indeed my biological father, something I had not known in my early years, and this came with the revelation of a new family too. (I will explain this further into the book.)

But for now, here I was in this little church hearing and experiencing a love from God that I had never experienced before.

The song being sung reached a crescendo with the words "I will go Lord if you lead me, I will hold your people in my heart." My sobs came in wave upon wave of release. Tears and love born from my feelings of such unworthiness.

"Why have you chosen me to shower this beautiful love on?" I did not feel I was able to deserve it.

Then as this new feeling spread throughout my being I began to yearn for others to experience this love that had just been planted in my heart. I began to say over and over in my mind.

"Send me, send me"

It was as if I wanted to tell the whole world about this feeling of love that had touched my heart in such a tangible way.

Dani looked at me with a slightly annoyed expression, borne I think of embarrassment at my loud crying. She said *"What's wrong with you?"*

"I don't know Dani, I just can't stop crying. I feel like I need to become a vicar and help people!"

We both laughed, and as I wiped away my tears I knew something had happened to me and I felt different!

As we walked back to the apartment, I was reminded about that day before my fortieth birthday, when I was weeping quietly at the retreat in Spain and asking God to prove His existence to me. Now, less than a month later He had done so and in such an amazing tangible way! I had indeed slayed the dragon! It was only as I stepped into all that this meant, that I slowly began to realise how clearly my Father God had been calling me and drawing me to Him and how the devil had been using his evil tactics to pull me into a world of darkness and death through destructive relationships based on my inability to understand and accept wholeheartedly the powerful effect of my heavenly Father's love for me.

The next day I drove back home after this amazing experience. My mind reflected on my life as it had been. I was suddenly reminded of a night when I was a little girl.

I had an extremely vivid dream, a dream I have never forgotten. I dreamt I was in our house on my own. All the windows were covered in black, as though they had literally been blacked out. As I wandered outside and saw there was no one about, I felt terribly alone. I looked up and saw a man with a long white beard, wearing a long white robe and holding a long stick in his hand like a tree branch. There was a ledge which travelled horizontally from left to right as far as I could see and along the edge of this ledge, looking down, right at me, were thousands of people! The white bearded man was within the centre of them all. He looked down at me. At that moment I awoke. I had been terrified that I was on my own. Years later as I was reading the account of Abraham in the

I further read in Isaiah 51:1-2

> *"Listen to me, you who pursue righteousness,*
> *who seek the LORD:*
> *Look to the rock from which you were hewn*
> *and to the quarry from which you were dug.*
> [2] *"Look to Abraham your father*
> *And to Sarah who gave birth to you in pain;*
> *When he was but one I called him,*
> *Then I blessed him and multiplied him.*

I realised years later that God was with me even as a small child and knowing at the right time I would be reminded that my wonderful Father in heaven is the God of Abraham, Isaac and Jacob. I am part of His family.

Arriving back home from Dani's, I went straight to my bedroom, because I knew I had a bible on my book shelf. It had been given to me by a wonderful Christian lady called Davina way back in August 1999. Davina was one of my regular beauty therapy clients who had left with her husband and gone to live in Canada. Her husband had been offered a place at a Bible College there. At the time that she gave me the bible, I had been dealing with so many problems, including Stuart being in prison, my depression, my two girls dealing with a myriad of issues at school. My eldest daughter was also struggling with depression. I was treading water. I'd had no interest in this God Davina was telling me about, but I liked Davina. She was a tiny young woman with a soft gentle voice, who seemed to really care about me. I appreciated her and her husband coming to see me and before they left they gave me a red leather bound bible, a 'New American Standard Version' whatever that meant. They prayed for me as well. I had been suffering with a recurring neck problem, possibly due to the stress I was under. As they put a gentle hand on my neck and back, they began to pray for healing. There was an intense heat radiating from my neck down my spine and into my lower back. I was quite amazed. I can honestly say I was healed and have never suffered from that problem again.

Now, here I was after having experienced God in a church in Brighton and four years after being given this bible, I was literally blowing the dust off the book they had given to me all those years ago; the book that had been sitting on my shelf throughout all that time, but had never been opened. I held the book in my right hand as if in a court room and about to give evidence. I sat on my bed and said,

"Dear God if all this is true, if you are real and do exist show me something in this book right now."

I randomly opened up the pages of the book and my eyes alighted on these words, which shocked me so much, that if I had not been sitting down, I would have fallen down!

The words said,

"Awake, awake, Deborah, awake, awake, sing a song!". The NIV version says *"Wake up, wake up Deborah"*

I was wide awake now and my Father God had my full attention!

Over the next few weeks, every time I thought about my heavenly Father I began to feel excited!

I had to stop attending the church that I'd shared with the vicar for my own sanity and, the little dignity I felt I had left. I began to attend a little village church just fifteen minutes away from where I lived. There, I became friends with a wonderful man called Chris. Chris is a member of a large Evangelical organisation, he very much supported me as I was possibly the youngest person in the congregation.

At that time I also threw away all of my books on subjects of study like the I Ching, crystal dowsing and self-esteem work books. I knew these books were taking me away from the love that God as my Father wanted to reveal to me. This was a revelation that came quite quickly. These were the very books, which due to their 'mystical' content, had held me in diverted interest, just as visiting my old friend who was the clairvoyant.

I understand some people might cringe at throwing books away. Looking back it was these very books that I read that made me realise they were not the way of bringing hope and life and creativity. Unfortunately, I did not have someone at the time to guide me to Jesus so it took longer to reach peace and love in my life. I was taken down wrong routes which led me away from God but paradoxically led me to God. I would make big decisions while dowsing, which on reflection always led me to darker pathways of life and were quite wrong leading me to choices based on whether the crystal on the end of the string would swing right or left. I'm not negating the power of dowsing; it is powerful. Powerfully dangerous! It's a way of walking in dark occult areas, allowing a false spirit to lead one's life. The bible clearly states that any kind of divination is prohibited and I can entirely understand why!

I also had real difficulty in letting go of my Buddha statues and crystals that I had collected in order to bring me luck and energy. They had cost me a lot of money, so I thought I would store them in the garage for the time being. Maybe it was ok to have these things in the house?

One Sunday I attended church and sat next to Chris, my friend.

We chatted before the start of the service and he began to tell me the story of a young friend of his whom he had visited the day before. Whilst he was there helping to move some furniture, he had noticed statues of Buddha's and boxes of crystals in the garage. He told me that he had told his friend in a gentle, matter of fact way,

"My dear, you need to destroy these things. They are like false gods and will keep you from receiving all that God has for you."

I felt my heart race, *"Chris, I've got stuff like that in my garage too!"*

"Well", he said *"Maybe God is letting you know the truth about this situation too"*. He gave me a wise look and I knew he had heard from the Holy Spirit.

Note :

It seems we are attracted to the mystical as a way of that innate sense of yearning that God has created within us to yearn for Him. These yearnings can initially lead us into the darker, mystical arenas and the occult, whilst we are exploring and finding our way to the real treasure, that of God's pure love.

I recall a time a few years later as a youth leader, (I will expound on this later in the book) I once was approached by a young girl whose best friend had committed suicide the year before. She was still bereft at his death and had been trying to contact him. She spoke to me about how she was angry and upset that he just left her, but also that she missed him. Her pain was very real; she sobbed uncontrollably as she opened up her heart to me after a year of bottling up those emotions. She was not a Christian, so I used a way of bringing the mystical to meet God at the point of her need. I arranged for her and her friends to meet at the church the next day. About thirty young people came with her on that day to help and support her as we went through the ritual of giving her some closure on her grief. I had asked her to write a letter or poem to her friend. On entering the church we all sat in a circle on the floor and I prayed and asked Jesus to be a real presence with us. I had lit a candle and it was placed in the middle of the circle. In a simple ceremony the young girl wept as did her friends as she read a poem out about her friend. Then she read out a letter she had written to him, she had stated all her pain and suffering at his choice to take his life. She was giving voice to her pain. Her friends wept with her and some of the friends prayed, at my invitation, they chose to ask God to look after him. I read a scripture from the book of Isaiah which I also printed out for her to keep. We then proceeded to leave the building, with the lighted candle. The girl said goodbye to her friend as she burned the letter and the ashes carried on the wind. It was all very symbolic and meant a great deal to the whole group, who went off skipping, full of joy after this short ceremony. What was it that created that yearning for closure? We have to acknowledge our pain and find a way to release it. I think if the young girl had gone to a clairvoyant she would have been told he was happy now, but what about all the hurt and grief for herself. Jesus healed her that day.

Chris had felt that I would also give their church a message and sure enough, within a month, I decided as lovely as all the people were, the church itself was just not alive. I was not excited about going to church. It felt incredibly boring to be honest.

Before I left he had helped me to rid my life of the things from my past by explaining they were stopping me from receiving all that Father wanted to give me. I burned the large wooden statue and smashed crystals; I also burned stuff from my past. I gave away to charity shops, all the items from my past that had been 'ill-gotten gains' and were not mine to have. I said sorry to God for the things I'd obtained through devious means and made a decision to be as honest as I could be. Over the years my family know I won't even accept so much as a pirate copy of the latest film! I've always said to my family, if you steal it reveals that you cannot trust God to provide for all of your needs.

After leaving this church behind, I asked Father to show me where to go as I had no idea and felt a little lost to be truthful. I was used to watching God TV to get as much teaching as I could about Jesus. One day shortly after seeking the Lord, I was travelling through a nearby village. I saw a sign outside a church, it was about an 'Alpha' Course. The banner said "Who is Jesus? Since my encounter with God in the July, I was hungry to know as much as I could about my Father God, Jesus and the Holy Spirit. I signed up for the course.

It was at this Alpha Course that I met the most amazing lady and a mighty woman of God. Her name is Jane, and she is still as much a part of my life now, as she was then. She was my small group leader. She volunteered her time to help us understand about the Christian faith in our small groups. I loved attending these sessions!

We would start the evening with a hot meal followed by a short presentation of topics such as 'Who is God? Who is Jesus? What is the Holy Spirit?' We would get into our small groups to discuss and debate this topic.

In John 16:7 Jesus promises that when He goes, in His place He is going to send the Holy Spirit to us. The Holy Spirit is the third person of the Trinity and Jesus promises the Spirit will guide us in to all truth John 16:13 Jesus says "But when He, the Spirit of truth comes, He will guide you into all the truth; for He will not speak on His own initiative, but whatever He hears, He will speak and He will disclose to you what is to come.

John 16:7 Jesus says,

"But very truly I tell you, it is for your good that I am going away. Unless I go away, the Advocate will not come to you; but if I go, I will send him to you"

On the tenth week we went on the 'Holy Spirit' weekend away.

The two days were teaching on 'Who is the Holy Spirit?' At the end of the first day we were all asked if we wanted to be filled with the Holy Spirit. There were over 200 people in that room led by the Dean of the Cathedral. Suddenly we were standing to our feet and I closed my eyes and waited to be given the Holy Spirit. A lovely lady who was part of the team there came and laid her hand on my shoulder came and prayed with me. She said,

"Debra, the Holy Spirit is giving you a spirit of evangelism"

Electricity flowed through my body! I felt such joy and peace and excitement all at the same time! I felt that I was waiting for something so delightful, my tummy had butterflies, and it was hope, real hope! I cried, then I laughed. I laughed so much that I couldn't stop and I had tears of joy streaming down my face. It was wonderful!

Even after that experience, I went home and in the quietness of my room began to ask *"Father God, is that real? Is the Holy Spirit really in me now?"* Again, I 'dipped in' to my Bible and this time the pages opened at the book of Galatians. What I read made me weep; how could Father God love me so much that he gave me such a precious gift?

The words were from the book of Galatians 6:17-18

"From now on let no one cause trouble for me, for I bear on my body the brand-marks of Jesus. The grace of our Lord Jesus Christ be with your spirit brethren. Amen"

I wrote at the bottom of the page '16th November 2003 day after the Holy Spirit day!'

It was at this time I was having clear dreams and I began to write down the details. In one dream I was working in a large house; it was a children's home. I knew that I could not allow the children to just go out of the front door or they would have been killed. Instead, I had to lead them through many passages within the house and finally to an escape hatch in the attic roof. In the dream I was really afraid for these children and I was careful to make sure I could guide them all through.

A week later my dear friends Dorcas and Simon called me to say there was an advert for a support worker in a Christian residential drug rehabilitation centre. The rehab was for young men with drug and alcohol addictions, and their ages ranged from 18-50 years old. When Dorcas and Simon were telling me I began to feel fearful; how could I possibly go from self-employed beauty therapist to drugs worker? I had no qualifications in that field. However the post was only part time, so after thinking it over, I decided to contact the company by telephone and asked for an application form. I was told it would be more than part time hours and I recall feeling disappointed and saying actually that I would probably not be able to do long hours due to having to look after my daughters as well. I was told to come in anyway and to see what happened.

I went for the interview and got the job! I worked part time for one week, then started full time hours, which continued for the rest of the time I worked there.

By this time, I was also attending a Sunday evening service at the nearby Cathedral. I was soon arranging to take some of the young lads from the rehab to the Sunday service and a handful came along. It was quite amusing to see them all rush off for showers and preen themselves, in preparation and hope of catching the eye of some young pretty female who happened to attend the service. One young man decided to come after hearing that there were girls at the service. He came down the stairs of the rehab with greased back hair and wearing a cravat and smart red herring bone jacket. We all laughed and as one of the others wolf whistled, another called out,

"Ding Dong" as if to be very impressed by his attire.

We all laughed as he held his head high and walked out of the door with an air of grace and charm!

Years later, I met up again with this lovely man, who was now in a wheel chair suffering with Motor Neuron disease. I hope the times he spent with us at the rehab allowed him to know the Lord.

I discovered that the rehab had been involved with the Cathedral in the past and although this was no longer the case, together with some of my fellow Christian workers we managed to get the guys there. At one Sunday service I realised my dream about the children's home had come to pass. The home was the rehab full of young men all behaving like children. If they decided to give up (some did, they couldn't face a life without these drugs) and walk out they would most inevitably face relapsing back into their drug addiction and possibly death, both physically and spiritually. But God was using me to lead these men through the passages of darkness towards the wonderful light of Christ.

One such man is Kel, a great friend of mine to this day and a mighty man of God. He had arrived at the local train station one wet and cold day, taking all the admin staff by surprise. No funding or other arrangements had been put in place for him; we had no paper work at all! My manager asked me to fetch him from the station, saying that if we couldn't get funding we would have to put him on a train back to London.

As I pulled in to the car park at the station, Kel stood out a mile! Dirty and disheveled, a tall, thin man, with a dirty horse hair coat, knee length white shell suit trousers and trainers with no socks. The first thing he did when I asked him if his name was Kel, was to hand over to me a pen knife.

"This is all I have on me, you'd better take it." It was indeed all he had on him. This man was broken and my heart went out to him.

Now, here we were some three months later, having secured his paper work and funding, and never knowing the Lord, Kel became one of my regular church attenders. He was eager to go each week! One week I knelt by his side in the church service,

"Lord" I said. *"Please will you have mercy on Kel? He is trying so hard to find you, please don't make it any more difficult for him"* My heart ached as I prayed for him. Suddenly he turned round and said,

"Did you just pray for me?"

"Yes, I did Kel"

"I know you did" he said, and as if confirming it to me, he said, *"I've just been touched by God through your prayer"*

Then as if to affirm me in my work the Lord reminded me of that song that I heard so clearly on the day the Lord spoke to me at that church in Brighton. Now here in the cathedral the voices of the people sang out again,

"Here I am Lord, is it I Lord? I have heard you calling in the night, I will go Lord if you Lead me I will hold your people in my heart"

Here now, holding Kel in my heart.

Kel has gone on in his faith and is very proactive with the poor and needy, setting up a project to help feed and clothe people. Kel was actually baptised at the same time as me at the Cathedral in May 2006. My claim to fame is that I was the first person to be baptised inside a cathedral in this country and I was baptised by my lovely friend who also prayed for the Holy Spirit to indwell in me, and the canon at the time who went on to greater things.

In the early days at the rehab, I had a vision. I was smoking at the back staff entrance on one of my breaks as I looked over the huge gardens.

(I had been a smoker since the age of 14, but after much prayer, I just gave up and have never smoked again, being healed and set free from this horrible addiction praise God!)

Suddenly I saw a tent being pitched on the huge, lawned area at the side of the house. A few weeks later I approached the Dean at the time of the cathedral, at one of the cathedral praise services.

"Do you fancy coming to the rehab and doing a service there for us please?"

"Have you asked any of the others?" He replied *"I'm a bit busy"*

"Well, actually, it's you the guys relate to, but not to worry"

I felt a bit indignant that he'd said that; too busy, I thought, we're all too busy, but if someone asks for help I'm sure we should try to do what we can. Little did I know at the time that he was the Dean of the cathedral, something I was soon to discover? (I was still getting used to all the hierarchy positions within the Anglican set up!) His lovely PA at the time told me that people have to book sometimes two years in advance to get him to visit.

Of course being the gentle man and mighty man of God that he is, looked intently at me and said

"Of course I will do it"

On that day the team came and set up a tent in the garden for the musicians. Over seventy people heard the Gospel and sang praises to God. My vision had come to pass.

There was a man called Calum who worked as a volunteer for the rehab. He had originally been there in recovery, but now, after being clean for ten years, he was able to escort residents to their various appointments or make up the staff numbers for outings. Calum would attend the praise services and, although he said he didn't believe in God, he seemed to want to be part of the team and join in the church services.

I began to feel an attraction for Calum and we would meet on my Saturdays off and go for breakfast, spending the day out together, going for walks in the nearby parks and chatting over coffee. We were good friends.

Regarding a relationship with anyone, I was very careful not to embark on any intimate relationship with any man. I knew that my life was so changed now; I had changed from being that woman who felt she desperately needed to be loved by any man. A relationship wouldn't define who I was anymore and now I had no desire to be needed by any man! I was no longer alone; I had the living Jesus guiding and leading me by the power of the Holy Spirit. The last thing I wanted was to get married! I was having great fun and joy discovering where my true identity lay. It was with Jesus as part of God's creation.

Calum and I had discussed a possible relationship and what would be acceptable to each other with regards to personal choices, likes and dislikes. He stated that if I planned to embark on any missions trips, (which was something I felt in my heart was another avenue for me to venture down) he wouldn't want me to do that. This set off alarm bells for me and I wasn't sure if he was right for me. I sought the Lord for his advice. Again I dipped in to my Bible.

*****Note: When I refer to 'dipping in', it really is a personal thing between myself and God. To really get to know God personally, actually putting in the time to study God's Word is vital*****

I read this passage from the book of Job:

Job 14: 1-6

'Man born of woman is of few days and full of trouble. He springs up like a flower and withers away; like a fleeting shadow he does not endure. Do you fix your eye on such a one? Will you bring him in judgment? Who can bring what is pure from impure? No one!

Man's days are determined; you have decreed the number of his months and have set limits he cannot exceed.

So look away from him and let him alone, till he fulfils his days like a hired man'

This certainly wasn't looking like I was getting the green light from God! I sensed that Calum was not the man God intended for me to be partnered with. We both agreed that we would stay friends and that taking our relationship on to a marriage commitment level was not good for either of us.

Once I left my work at the rehab and also because of my new relationship, (see later) our paths separated quite quickly.

I have not seen my dear friend for quite some years now. He chose a path that is not good for his life. I continue to pray for him.

The relationship with my Father in heaven has developed in a deeper way and further to that, my reliance on Him increases as I look to Him for guidance through the power of the Holy Spirit; always referring back to His Word to guide me.

CHAPTER 4

The Mission -Into Obedience

Luke 10:1-12 The Message

Later the Master selected seventy and sent them ahead of
him in pairs to every town and place where he intended
to go. He gave them this charge:

"What a huge harvest! And how few the harvest hands. So
on your knees; ask the God of the Harvest to send harvest
hands.

3 *"On your way! But be careful—this is hazardous work.*
You're like lambs in a wolf pack.

4 *"Travel light. Comb and toothbrush and no extra*
luggage.

"Don't loiter and make small talk with everyone you meet
along the way.

> *5-6 "When you enter a home, greet the family, 'Peace.' If your greeting is received, then it's a good place to stay. But if it's not received, take it back and get out. Don't impose yourself.*
>
> *7 "Stay at one home, taking your meals there, for a worker deserves three square meals. Don't move from house to house, looking for the best cook in town.*
>
> *8-9 "When you enter a town and are received, eat what they set before you, heal anyone who is sick, and tell them, 'God's kingdom is right on your doorstep!'*
>
> *10-12 "When you enter a town and are not received, go out in the street and say, 'The only thing we got from you is the dirt on our feet, and we're giving it back. Did you have any idea that God's kingdom was right on your doorstep?' Sodom will have it better on Judgment Day than the town that rejects you'*

In September of 2004, Chris had invited me to join the mission being organised by the evangelical organisation. There were plans for a mission trip to Torquay in Devon, a year later, in September 2005. I agreed with Chris that I would go for a week of mission, which meant using a week of my annual holiday leave. It was a long time away and to be honest, I wasn't sure it would even happen. In the April of 2005, I had to travel to a training course overnight in Bristol. Not being the best route planner, I had looked at a map and decided the way to go was to turn left onto the M40 rather than right and onto the M5. I went the long way around much to my frustration which I only realised when I was half way down the M40! But reflecting upon this, I realise that God used this long journey to reveal more of His love for me. As

I was driving the sun was on my right and the brightness caught my eye. As I looked over towards it, it was as though the sun created the most amazing 'Cross' in a deep red hue in the sky with the bottom tip looking like it had rested on the setting sun. If I hadn't been driving I would definitely have taken a photograph! It was incredibly beautiful! I felt that the Lord was saying in my heart,

"I am giving you freedom like you have never experienced before. The cross is before you and the world behind you. Now is the time that your search for 'Me' is over. I am here. Now it is time to get to know Me"

Wow I was blown away by this revelation I felt such an excitement within me, I had not experienced such love, such hope, such life. Something had changed in me and I was filled with a great expectation of great things to come

Continuing my journey, I began to notice signs on the backs of various Lorries and trucks. One particular sign stood out to me on more than one occasion; *"Professional Logistics"*

The definition of logistics is the detailed coordination of a complex operation involving many people, facilities, or supplies. Logistics is involved in many different things and is used by many different people. There are different types of logistics

I began to understand and sense that God was involving me in a huge operation to help gather people to salvation through His love.

At one point on the journey, I lost my way and I was wondering if I should pull over and check my map when I noticed another lorry ahead of me, it had a picture of a large bunch of grapes on a vine on it and the words "Follow Me"! I decided by faith I would follow for a while and see if I could get back to a main road. Sure enough the lorry brought me right outside the place I needed to be!

I trained for the weekend and met some amazing fellow Christians. I felt that I was in the right place at the right time and this was where

I was meant to be. I was amazed that here I was mixing with other people who loved Jesus and I was with them being given teaching in how to develop my relationship with my Father, after all I had been through I knew I had truly found Him and more importantly He had found me!

In early June 2005 I came into work and was told my boss that a new worker was starting that day called Hugh. I was told that he would 'shadow me' for two weeks.

I was due to go on annual leave at the end of the two weeks and his role would be to take over my shift pattern while I was away. On the morning of June 5th 2005 I walked into the staff office for the morning hand over and I saw a tall man looking over at me. He wore blue jeans and a checked shirt. He had short greying hair and was about my age I reckoned. I did not acknowledge him as I was brought straight into the dramas of the previous night. Some of the residents had been causing trouble with one of the other workers, who wasn't a very strong character and she had complained they refused to follow the house rules. Once the hand-over was complete, Hugh McNeill came over to the desk where I was sitting and held out his hand whilst introducing himself. Bless him, I thought. He seems like a nice guy. Eventually I discovered he was at a low season in his life and we often ended up discussing where God was in his life. I tried to encourage him whenever I could. One day he asked me out for a drink. I wasn't sure really, I wanted to focus on the Lord and I didn't really need any distractions. He seemed too nice anyway and I wondered what was wrong with him. I had not had good experiences in the past so I felt better being on my own. However we did go out for a few drinks on occasions and that was nice. I didn't feel attracted to him, so it was just good to have the friendship with no expectations of me trying to impress him.

September 2005 and the Mission trip was about to begin in Torquay. On my last day of work, Friday, I had a full nine to five duty at the rehab and then I was to go and buy my train ticket for my journey the following day down to Torquay. I was travelling down on my own. It felt at the time, as though my heart just wasn't in it, and I believe if I'd been more expectant and excited about the trip, I would possibly have made travel arrangements with others and set the tone for an amazing time away, delivering the Gospel to all who needed to hear it.

I mention my heart, as that very day, I began to experience extremely severe chest pains whilst in work; so much so, that I was concerned enough to visit to the local hospital's A & E Department. I was rushed into a cubicle and blood tests, heart monitors and examinations were all duly ordered and started. I was quite bewildered. I began to ask God was going on? He did not reply. I began to watch all the people rushing by the cubicle and I thought the least I could do was to pray for others as they went past. I prayed for the doctors and nurses, the patients and their concerned carers and loved ones. Eventually I was moved to an observation ward and told that I had to stay till 5pm for the results of my blood tests as it was possible I may have suffered a stroke! As it was only lunch time I decided to make the most of this opportunity and I slept for a few hours. It was great; here was I, resting in a bed, far from the rehab, where I had left a scene of mayhem. One of the lads had started a situation and there was a huge meeting going on with lots of shouting and arguing. That's probably why I was feeling pain in my chest; all the stress of the day.

I soon discovered the little New Testament Bible on the side of the bed locker and began to read it. Matthew 11:28-30

> *'Come to Me, all who are weary and heavy-laden, and I will give you rest. Take My yoke upon you and learn from Me, for I am gentle and humble in heart; and you SHALL FIND REST FOR YOUR SOULS. For my yoke is easy and My load is light'*

I felt that God was telling me to just take it easy. Looking back I have come to realise the richness and fullness of those words. It is only when we can give all of ourselves into God's care can we live a life of peace and even joy in the midst of chaos. This takes time because we need to know someone enough to trust them with our lives. We can only learn to trust someone if we are prepared to get to know them and develop a relationship with them. This is what FATHER God is drawing us all to, to get to know who He is and how we can begin to see and understand who we are because of our relationship with him, after all he is our Creator He knows us best and He wants us to understand how fantastic we are and what we are capable of, it's a bit like getting a high powered top notch car like a Jaguar, then keeping it in the garage and using the old banger you have on the drive.

At precisely 5pm the doctor came to my bedside and informed me that the blood tests were clear and I was free to go. I tried to make sense of it all while I drove home.

The mission in Torquay was starting the next day and I began to make excuses in my mind why I shouldn't go. It was over 200 miles to get there and I really wasn't sure I should go.

"I need to be careful" I said to myself. After all, I nearly had a suspected heart attack!

I decided I would give this to the Lord.

"Lord, I'm not sure if today was a sign that you really don't want me to go on mission tomorrow? Lord, I have no train ticket (I really did not want to go the train station and buy a ticket after the day I had) If you really want me to go on mission tomorrow Lord then let someone offer to take me."

I had put my offer to Father on the table, if He wanted me there He would need to get someone to take me. Arriving home I made a small cup of tea and went off to bed with a hot water bottle. Even though there was nothing wrong with me physically I still determined to stay in the mindset that I needed to treat myself with kid gloves after all I could have had a heart attack! The girls were with their dad as I had arranged for them to be there for the next week.

As I lay in bed my text message alert sounded on my phone and it was Hugh. Our friendship had grown and we had become good friends. He had worked for three months at the rehab with me. Working with addicts is highly stressful; because of their addictions and at times, desperation, some can portray extremely manipulative traits and I experienced attacks on my personal life, at times when certain individuals couldn't bear to look at their own lives. It was very disheartening at times and I felt like some would 'pick holes' in my armour. I did get used to this and definately learnt quickly, the best approach with these young men.

Most of the men who were staying at the rehab had trouble with a male authority figure- most of them had not had good experiences of a father figure whether it was their own father or step-father. To be honest there was not one man who had come from a stable home life with loving parents. One man in particular swore blind that Hugh was an ex-prison officer who treated him badly. This was, of course, not true, but this man was like a dog with a bone and insisted Hugh was his ex-prison officer. Hugh decided, and quite rightly so for him at that time, that he would not accept a full time contract and he left to pursue his own business. He did however join the bank staff and worked shifts whenever he knew I was on duty!

On the final night of his employment with the rehab, we all arranged to meet at a local wine bar and night club. There was another member of staff leaving also; a lovely student who had been on a work experience initiative, and members of the permanent staff wanted to say goodbye. Hugh arrived late as he was working his last shift till 10pm. When he came into the wine bar he came and stood next to me whilst the other ladies I was with went off to dance. It was a bit of an awkward moment. I wasn't sure what to say to him. Finally Barry White's *'Can't get enough of your love'* started to play and a man standing on my left spoke into my ear,

"I really like this song" he said. I laughed and agreed. Hugh must have noticed this interaction and immediately took my hand and said,

"Would you like to dance with me?"

"Yes" I said.

As we danced together he said *"I was a bit worried that guy was going to ask you to dance; I thought I'd better get in quick!"*

We laughed and, I liked the fact that he wanted to 'fight' for me. On the way out of the bar, a woman was selling roses and he bought one for me. I smiled and thanked him, giving him a light kiss on the cheek. Then the three girls and I all headed for my house where they were staying. I said goodnight to Hugh and told him we would keep in touch. When we got home I put the rose in a vase on the window sill in front of the kitchen window. The next morning my daughter came downstairs and spotting the rose shouted *"Mum who gave you the rose?"*

"Oh....... nobody" I said as I smiled to myself.

Over the next few months we met now and again. I wasn't sure where this was heading and I wasn't sure if he was the one for me so I did play it cool. I knew he liked me and was always happy to meet up.

I'd now been single for nearly two years and I wasn't sure if I was really ready for a relationship. My last two marriages had not turned out to be good and I knew that if I was to date anyone it would be on the understanding that I was looking for a long term marriage partner. I would never be in the business of divorce because now I knew that God would direct my path to the right man. We went out on a lunch date, and I found Hugh to be such a pleasant man. He told me that he had separated from his wife and left Ireland where he had lived for the past thirty years. He was waiting for his divorce to come through. I was a bit bothered by this and decided I would take a bit of a back seat.

We met up every now and again and I have to say I did look forward to seeing him.

Now, as I lay in bed after my day in hospital, I read his text to me.

"Hi Deb, how was your day?"

I texted back.

"Ok now. I've been in hospital all day with chest pains, but they've let me come home now to rest" I replied. We women can be so dramatic sometimes!

The next moment my phone was ringing. Hugh sounded alarmed!

"Are you alright Deb? What happened?"

I gave him a full account of the day's events and told him that actually there was nothing wrong with me as I'd been given the all clear and the pains were possibly just stress.

He then said,

"Did you get your train ticket for tomorrow?"

"No, I just didn't get time Hugh" I said, *"by the time I got out of the hospital I just wanted to go home"*

Then it came. The confirmation of the Lord that I was to go!

"I can drive you down to Torquay, if you still want to go; I'd love to help!" Hugh offered.

Smiling up at heaven, I said,

"Yes I do want to go, it would be really great if you can take me."

I gave Hugh my address. Up to this point, I had not invited him into my home, so this was a big step for me.

Hugh arrived bright and early and we drove 200 miles to Torquay. We had a fabulous chat on the way down and I was almost sorry that he was leaving me there for a week. I actually felt I would miss him but I was also excited now too, as I mingled with approximately 200 men and women from the Through Faith Missions organisation.

I was put into a group of twelve others and we were driven by local church members to our church destination. This was to be our headquarters for the next week. I was invited in to the home of a lovely lady called Sharon. She lived on her own with her two little dogs. Her home was wonderful. It was perched tightly into the cliffs that surround the town of Torquay. High up we had a panoramic view of the coast line, and it was the most amazing view I had enjoyed in a long time. Sharon and I got on so very well and we often chatted away into the late night. I told her all about Hugh, saying I wasn't sure he was for me. I did speak to him each night even though spiritually it would have been better to leave the phone alone and focus on what God wanted me to do on this my very first mission. I prayed and asked God,

"Lord, is Hugh the right man for me?" Again, cheekily dipping into my Bible, my eyes alighted on these words from Zechariah 9:9

> *'Rejoice greatly, oh daughter of Zion! Shout in triumph o daughter of Jerusalem! Behold your king is coming to you; He is just and endowed with salvation, humble and mounted on a donkey'*

Now, this scripture is a Messianic message about Jesus, but to me at that time I felt the word was about Hugh; that he was a peaceful man; gentle and servant- hearted and that he was, indeed, the man for me. I kept this in my heart and did not share it.

The mission was going well. One morning, three of us had been invited to the local primary school to do a small teaching in a school assembly. This went very well and on leaving, we walked back down the hill, back towards the town centre and towards our church headquarters where we had been given the task of making lunch for the whole group. It was a lovely, sunny day and people would wave to us or say hello. We were recognised because we all wore the same distinct green polo shirts with the missions logo on the front and a transfer of a pair of men's boots on the back with a circled logo which read *'How beautiful on the mountains are the feet that bring good news'*

As we were entering the local shop to buy the lunch ingredients, I suddenly heard the voice of the Lord very clearly.

"Stay outside!" I knew it was meant for me, so I told the other girls I would wait outside for them. Next to the shop, there was a path that expanded to a large, paved area and, as I waited, a group of men appeared. I could tell from my own working experience that these men were all rough sleepers with some type of substance misuse addiction. They recognised the shirt I was wearing and one spoke;

"One of your lot prayed for us yesterday" a gap- toothed man proclaimed, as he broke into a smile, his teeth black and rotting. I smiled back and engaged them all in conversation.

"Where have you come from this morning?" I asked

"We sleep near the trees at the top of the town at night time and then come down into the town in the morning. Then we can go to the homeless project and get breakfast and hang out" said the gap-toothed gentleman

There was a lot of places that cared for these men in Torquay, It's such a sunshine kind of place who wouldn't want to live there? The Christian rehab where I worked had a sister project in a nearby town that offered residential accommodation for homeless men, but there was limited space. I intended to go and visit them to say 'hello' on my morning off the next day. There was also another homeless project which we were invited to visit later that day.

In the meantime, as we chatted in the sunshine, the other girls came out of the shop and we talked with each of the men, listening to their stories and hoping for another chance to speak about Jesus. I got talking to Jimmy, a tall thin man who did not look very well. He told me and my friend Steph, that he had been in hospital and had been discharged only recently. He was going to visit one of the projects to enquire about accommodation. We spoke to Jimmy for a while; he wanted to know why we had chosen to come here to talk about Jesus. One of the other ladies then invited Jimmy to take the opportunity to start a relationship with our living God; the Jesus who lives in us and guides us by the Holy Spirit into a real living relationship with Him.

Jimmy said *"What? A real relationship; where God speaks to you an' all?"*

"Yes" said the lady.

"Yes! I'd like to do that" said Jimmy.

The lady led Jimmy in a simple prayer; first of all thanking Jesus for his sacrifice on the Cross and then admitting his own wrong doings in his life; saying sorry and asking Jesus to lead him now in a life filled with the love of God. Jimmy's eyes sparkled! At that moment life seemed to stop; still, and we all wept. Our hearts burned within us as we looked upon this bedraggled, skinny man, with his sallow sunken skin. His grin was not a pretty sight, but we gazed lovingly at him as his eyes twinkled brightly, lighting up his whole face. I was so grateful that I had heard from God. It hadn't been often that God had spoken directly to me, but it seemed this was His mode of communication for me on that particular day, just like the day I heard His voice in that church in Brighton. Now, I had obediently followed his guidance to stay out of the shop. Had I gone into the shop; had I not been sensitive to the voice of God; the men would have walked straight past and Jimmy would not have made a commitment that day. (Some people think that just saying a simple prayer is not enough to be accepted into the Kingdom Of God, however as I recall the time I lay on the beauty couch back on my retreat in Spain crying out to God, I was desperate in my heart to find God, and He promises if we eagerly seek Him with our whole heart we will find him and He will heal us.) Jimmy wanted this relationship and the very act of making a move toward God and asking Him to take care of us, is in my opinion enough. It's then that a process of how we enjoy the enrichment of what all that means and how that develops in our lives with Jesus.)

The following day, I did visit the sister project and met the manager there. I was hoping Jimmy had been blessed enough to get a bed and so asked him if he knew Jimmy. He said he did and I told him that Jimmy had made a commitment to the Lord the day before. He then said to me,

"Jimmy died last night!"

The shock waves rippled through me. I suddenly realised the importance of my obedience to God. I was ashamed that I had tried to 'haggle' with God over my apathy to come on mission and here God was clearly revealing to me the fruit of my decision to come on this trip. I quickly repented and rejoiced that our brother Jimmy was no longer in pain and suffering but with our Lord Jesus Christ.

Later that day we went to visit the other homeless project. Our leader for that day was Roger, a great evangelist and wonderful man of God. He had never heard my testimony so I was able to share the story of my past, about my relationship with Stuart and the vicar; how I was saved from being murdered and, how God had called to me in church, that unforgettable day in Rottendean. One of the homeless girls said afterwards,

"Blimey, you could send that in to a magazine and get at least a hundred quid for that story!" We all laughed. I was touched by their warmth and love and blessed by their eagerness to please and share what they had with us.

They served us a lovely meal and we spent time laughing and conversing. I decided to sponsor the project for a time; I was so touched by the hard work from the staff and the way the people respected them for helping.

I had also been a bit foolish. We are told by faith not to bring any money with us only £2.00 to buy someone else a drink and bless them.

I however had bought a blank cheque. As I walked back to the church one evening I saw some of the homeless men sleeping in the porch way of the church, their wet socks dangling from the letter box on the church door in the hope that they would be dry by the next morning. I decided to go to a nearby popular store and purchased two sleeping bags and a tent for these two men. I was very proud of my offering. However one of the staff at the nearby soup kitchen told me the next day, they had taken the stuff back to the shop, got their money back and bought drugs with it!

Once Roger had heard my testimony, he asked me if I would tell my story at the service which was planned in the large local church on Sunday. I agreed. I hadn't ever spoken to a large crowd before, but I wanted to let everyone know how Jesus had saved me. On the Sunday I was invited to up to a large podium and I gave my testimony. Afterwards a man approached me, he seemed really angry,

"What did you forgive him for?" he said, *"You're an idiot! That man was going to murder you and you still loved him and forgave him. Stupid!"*

I replied, *"I can't help the way I felt. I did love him. I wouldn't have married him otherwise"*

The man, of course, was talking about Stuart. At the same time some of the church staff intervened and started defending my position. The man realised I was surrounded by a few people who had heard him ranting and so he backed off. Someone later told me that this man had himself murdered somebody and had recently left prison. He had been locked up for a long time. I guess my story was too close for comfort for him.

It was on this mission that I began to realise the differences in denominational churches. Each church we visited had a distinct community, which differed in each church. On our final day we were to go door to door with a questionnaire, inviting people to their local church. We decided to follow a main road which led away from the town centre and up a steep hill. I felt that we weren't where we were supposed to be and asked the small group if we could wait and pray for guidance. As we waited I could smell a strong odour, like gas. We had stopped outside a house and by their front wall the gas odour was thick and heavy in the air. I called the gas services and reported the leak as a matter of urgency. I gave the address and they said that they would send someone immediately. We knocked on the door of the house but no one was in. We decided we had done what we could to help and hopefully the gas services would soon be there. We felt we needed to move on, it was our last day and we needed to meet people.

We came across a small housing estate and walked through. As we began to knock on doors the whole neighbourhood seemed to spill out onto the small, grassy bank, which was set between the houses. It was almost like a courtyard area. These people were friendly and I think they all liked the fact that we had made the effort to come and see them. Each one of us sat on the grass telling the neighbours about Jesus and I gave my testimony. There was talk of others who had similar experiences, and then as if waiting on a queue, a little girl holding her skipping rope came up to me. Our eyes were level as I was sat on the grass. Looking at me intently she said,

"You came to our school assembly didn't you?"

"Yes we did" I replied. I smiled and she put the handle of her skipping rope in her mouth and chewed it slightly. I could tell she was pondering on her thoughts. Then she said,

"Have you come to help us?"

"I've come to tell you about Jesus and how He can help you" I said. Our small group sat on the grass that day and chatted about Jesus. A young man who seemed to be the leader of the people said to us,

"We've asked for help from that big church down there, but no one helps us," he said.

"What help are you looking for?" I asked

"We want to turn the old hall down there into a church and community centre because there's nothing for us up here"

I told them I was disappointed they felt the church had not supported them and I would be speaking to the local church leaders before I left to see what support they could possibly offer their little community. The small crowd allowed us to pray with them and then we left, blessing them with God's love before we went on our way. Two of the group relayed to us on the way back about how they had gone into the home of an old man who was quite clearly depressed. They did tell an agency on their return. This man had been so glad they came and he too had given his life to Jesus. We don't know what happened to this man only that Jesus visited him that day through our work of teaching others about the love of Jesus Christ.

Roger was travelling back to our home town and I asked him if I could possibly travel with him, in order to return home. We chatted in the car and I recalled to him some of the stories from the other mission friends I'd made. I really felt energised and full of joy. I told Roger about Hugh as I'd asked Roger to drop me off at a petrol station near my home. Hugh had offered to pick me up from there. Roger offered to take me home but I told him Hugh would be waiting. I had said that Hugh and I were just friends and Roger smiled. He said,

"It's a good friend indeed who drives you all the way to Torquay, drops you off and comes straight home again!"

We both laughed and deep down inside I was just a little bit excited to be seeing Hugh again!

Over the next two years Hugh and I dated on and off. I wasn't sure how I truly felt and due to my past experiences I was apprehensive about committing myself to another relationship. I understood now about marriage and commitment and, whereas in the past the divorce card always seemed a 'get out' clause for me, now it was vital that if I were to marry it would be for as long as either of us had breath in our bodies. Looking back, I realise that without Hugh in my life, I would have struggled to stay sane, as the future was suddenly about to become extremely tough.

Little did I know it at the time, but God was promoting me for my obedience and love for Him over the past few years and now I was about to begin a new season in the wilderness. This happens, not because God wants to punish us, but because He wants us to discover more of who we are in Him; discover our true identity, which is revealed by Him, who has created us. In other words, if God has a magnificent plan for our lives, He certainly wants us to see all of what He has for us. He calls us on and when we are ready he allows challenges to come our way so that we can press in to Him. We are put in situations that we have no control over, but have to totally rely on God and, when we do, He demonstrates His love and blesses us with more of how wonderfully He has made us! We are pushed gently to take risks and see exponential growth in our spirit and our lives and we can! Satan means situations and circumstances to occur for our harm and distress, but Gods promise in Romans 8:28 is this:

> *'And we know that God causes all things to work together for good to those who love God, to those He called according to His purpose'*

After the Torquay mission, I returned to work. I guess the devil wanted pay back for my mission work; for the lives, especially Jimmy's that had been saved by my compulsion and that of the other missionaries; telling others of the love of Jesus that in turn had saved us too. I also believe that what I went through enabled me to become an overcomer of those dark times and develop a deeper relationship with God. You see, when it seems that all around you is going totally wrong in your life, it's always a sign that God is right there with you, and wants you to take hold of a fresh perspective of His love for you. The more we have to rely on God the more we can develop a deeper relationship with Him as He reveals so much more about how He loves us and wants so desperately to take care of us. If I was to offer any wisdom to the reader I would say this;

"When times are tough and you seem in a dark place, the way to get out is to sing, yes sing songs of thanksgiving to God. Sing songs that reveal how you would expect God to bless you in this darkness to move out into light and love, His joy and peace. Once you leave this earth you will never have the opportunity to give such a sacrifice to God because He tells us there is no more sorrow and tears in eternity so we do it now while we have the opportunity! It is a real sacrifice when you are in a dark place and you don't want to sing JOYOUSLY TO THE LORD, but that is exactly the time that you should, so you can prevent satan from having his way in your misery. Give it to God instead. He will turn that situation around and you will praise Him.

CHAPTER 5

Moving into the Kingdom - stepping up

At the end of April 2006 I was the first person ever to baptised by full immersion (Being put in under the water rather than a sprinkle) in a Cathedral in the United Kingdom. I was sprinkled as a baby, but I knew in my spirit that I needed to be baptised; cleansed and renewed.

> *Matthew 3:5-6*
>
> *'Then Jerusalem was going out to him (John the Baptist) and all Judea and all the district surrounding Jordan. And they were being baptised by him in the Jordan River as they confessed their sins'*

I decided I would step out in faith, take a risk and see what God wanted to reveal to me. I put a fleece out to my heavenly Father.

> Judges 6
>
> *'Gideon said to God, 'If you will save Israel by my hand as you have promised – 37 look, I will place a wool fleece on the threshing-floor. If there is dew only on the fleece*

> *and all the ground is dry, then I will know that you will save Israel by my hand, as you said.' 38 And that is what happened. Gideon rose early the next day; he squeezed the fleece and wrung out the dew – a bowlful of water.*
>
> *39 Then Gideon said to God, 'Do not be angry with me. Let me make just one more request. Allow me one more test with the fleece, but this time make the fleece dry and let the ground be covered with dew.' 40 That night God did so. Only the fleece was dry; all the ground was covered with dew.*

I love the fact that Gideon was just like the majority of human beings; one proof of God showing His love to us is not enough we feel, and we need to keep on seeing it. And why not? God loves us so much, He is desperate to show us all the time! It's ourselves who need to keep asking for guidance and wisdom. (James 1:5) but once we truly understand our identity; who we are in Him and, how we have been created by God, we can begin to totally trust God for everything in our lives. Without Him we begin to realise there is nothing in our world worth having; treasures that will rust away, are all we can store up when we don't have faith in Jesus.

I had been sensing that my time at the rehab was coming to an end and I felt so strongly that I was about to move in some way into a new season that God had been preparing me for.

So, I decided to put a fleece out, as I had given my life to Father God and I wanted to know what He wanted me to do. I told Him I was putting my house up for sale and if it sold within one month I would go wherever he wanted me to go.

The baptism came at the end of April and by the end of May the house was sold! After years of putting it on the market and it never getting sold, now was the right time, Holy Spirit putting that yearning on my heart to go and preach the gospel of Jesus Christ. I was ready and felt strongly it was time to give my notice in at work, freeing myself to go and do what Father wanted me to do.

Here is an amazing example of how God works all things for good if you just let him. Trying to make things happen isn't always wise. We must wait for guidance by the Holy Spirit.

Once the house was sold, I decided I would write my letter of resignation to the rehab centre. I no longer felt passion for this work as I had done previously and, in fact, looking back on this time, I see I was really burnt out. I had been there for two years and had worked very hard, giving all I had. I did not regret a minute of it and the Lord was able to impact people's lives through my work. Some of the men accepted Jesus Christ into their lives and this has led some into a completely new life, clean from drugs and addiction. I have since gone on to attend many weddings of these men getting married to Godly women and taking the Gospel to some of the darkest places imaginable where they have been able to share their darkest experiences and bring light into others' lives.

The letter of resignation was forgotten three mornings in a row; just left on the table in the dining room. On the fourth day, my manager told me that someone from the Human Resources Department (Personnel), would be coming to speak to us all the next day. He quietly told me he felt there may be redundancies coming up! I was so pleased I hadn't put in my notice as I would have missed out on any redundancy pay. The news soon spread around the centre; all of the staff were being made redundant as the centre was going to be transformed into a 'Twelve-Step' Programme centre and managed by 12-Step trained staff. As we were not trained in 12-Step, we had the opportunity to take a lower grade position as a project worker but this would mean a drastic cut in salary.

At the start of my new life with Jesus, I began to have quite a few dreams which seemed almost life like. One night I dreamt I was walking down a road. On one side there were fields and the other side houses. Water was pouring off the fields onto the road. As I went to the bottom of the road, there were young people all being baptised in baths. I felt the place was called Leamington. I met a man walking down the road and I recognised him as someone I knew; it was my dear friend Morris. He said to me in the dream,

"You will go all the way around and come back again"

One of the roads was signposted Rectory Drive.

At this time and, as part of the redundancy process, I was offered a new position as deputy manager for the rehab organisation in Bournemouth with higher wages and a whole new beginning! Was this where I was being called to?

As I was considering this, out of the blue, my dear friend Dorothy called me about a position she had seen in the Church Times newspaper, advertising for a Youth and Community worker with the chance of completing a BA Degree in Youth and Community and Applied Theology. Along with doing the full time course, I would also have to work part-time in a little village! Could this be my dream? I reflected on my notes about the dreams I had been having and this seemed to resonate with me.

A BA Degree with honors! Here was I, born on a council estate in the poorer end of town, coming out of school with very few qualifications and now I was about to embark on a degree! I was confident I could do this. I saw that the closing date was only one day away. Not having a computer at that time, I zoomed off to my local library and began the task of filling in the form. I was not computer literate so I knew everything that I did would be double the time. I'd spoken to the vicar and told him I would be applying. I prayed, asking God to close all the doors that weren't of Him and to open the right doors for me. That day I also took a run over to Whitnash to take a look at the place. As I drove past St. Margaret's Church I turned immediately first left into a small estate thinking I could catch a glimpse of the back of the church. There on one side was a road called 'Rectory Lane', and the right was 'Morris Avenue'. Whitnash is a suburb of Leamington Spa!! My dream had turned out to be quite prophetic!

The next day, on the closing date for the position, the vicar at St. Margaret's telephoned,

"We haven't received your application form as yet and wondered are you still interested in applying?"

I was shocked! I thought I'd sent it? I went back to the library and resent the form and this time the application was received. I was invited to an interview on 9th June, but I had to decline as I was going on a mission to a place called Accrington with Through Faith Missions. I thought the vicar would think I was messing about and with lack of faith I assumed they would decline my application but that didn't happen. Returning from the mission I was offered an interview. It also happened at the same time I was being offered an interview for the job in Bournemouth, and I wasn't sure. I decided to wait and see if I got the Whitnash post. When I told Jade I might take a job in Bournemouth, she got really upset and asked me not to go so far away from her. I felt that I had let them down, still feeling guilt and shame for my choice to divorce their father and remarry a stranger. Now, I wanted to do things the right way. I was trying to focus on what I thought God was calling me to do.

I got the post with St. Margaret's. I received the news just as I had come out of a meeting with the area directors of the organisation for the Bournemouth post. They had just arranged for me to go down and check out the place. They were even organising my travel. Knowing how Jade felt and then getting the 'yes' for Whitnash, I went straight back to the directors and turned down the offer for Bournemouth. I never regretted that at all. If anything it confirmed to me that they valued me as an employee and that reflected in the fact that the position offered was one of management.

By the time I'd accepted the post at St. Margaret's, it was late June and I now realised I had to apply for the degree course. I'd never experienced the process and was overwhelmed by the computer work and report writing I had to do just in order to complete the clearing process to apply to a University! The church I would be working for were paying for the degree. Here I was, just a council estate kid, doing a degree. I was a bit scared to be honest, but if God calls you into something, it is He who opens the door and no one can shut it!

I took a huge risk and bought a house in Whitnash by faith before I knew if I'd been accepted on the course. In late July 2006 I went for an interview to Christian Youth Ministries (CYM) who were running the course which was to start in the September. On the day I was to attend, I was to bring evidence of my NVQ 3 in Health Care as proof that I could do the academic work. That came in the post that very day and I was able to give the administration department a copy of that certificate on the day of my interview. Unbeknown to me at the time, CYM were going to offer me a place the following academic year 2007, due to my late application. I was told this at my exit interview when I had completed my degree. The reason they changed their mind was that when I had attended the initial interview I had informed the interviewer (just as I was walking out of the door) that I had already, by faith, purchased a house in the town, where I would be working as part of the degree requirements. The committee decided to allow me to join the 2006 interns.

So, I was accepted to study for a degree in Youth & Community and Applied Theology with Oxford Brookes University through Christian Youth Ministries. The place was funded by St. Margaret's Church in Whitnash where I was accepted as the new part time youth worker and the degree was part of this work. I was blessed that through the balance of the sale of the house I was able to buy a house outright with no mortgage or rent to pay. I was a very rich student!

In early August of 2006, I said my 'Goodbyes' at the rehabilitation centre and moved out of the family home I had shared with my first husband and my daughters. The new owners were kind enough to let me store my furniture in the garage as I was not able to complete the legalities on the new house in Whitnash until the end of August. The day I moved out my best friend Dee let me move in with her until I could occupy the new house. As I walked away from my old home, with my little dog Zig and a few things in a suitcase, I cried. My heart was achingly lonely; Catherine was living in the North of England and Jade with her Dad. I said goodbye to a home I'd lived in for fifteen years. I was now living with the consequences of my past actions and choices. It seemed to me, I had dislocated my family and now, I was also leaving the place I'd called home for over 15 years. When I arrived at Dee's house, she was out at work. I put my belongings in the little box room where I would be sleeping. I felt like a fish out of water.....what had I done? I was extremely scared and completely out of my comfort zone.

I had also stopped dating Hugh. I felt I wasn't ready to become involved again and I wanted to concentrate on my new start. I didn't feel it was right to arrive at my new place as the youth worker, dating a man I wasn't married to. That seems silly now in reflection, but that was my naivety. So, my only friend at that time was my lovely Dee, who I could share my painful heart with over a bottle of red wine, on my first night in her home.

Once all the conveyancing matters were sorted I was given the keys to the first home of my own. It was late August 2006. I was now a resident of Whitnash the tiny suburb of Leamington Spa. No sooner was I there, than my first summer school mission with the evangelical organisation began, lasting a week. On my return, I had one week at home then my studies began with fresher's week at University. I had now stepped into the new season of my life and things just got tougher.

At the time of starting the course my daughter Catherine was beginning to become a real concern. She was not well and her health was not good. Her partner Tim was trying to help but she was weak and needed nurturing. I prayed and asked God what was to be done, I was worried for health. But as I spoke to God I understood He was going to send them both back my way.

> *Jeremiah 24:6-7 'For I will set my Eyes on them for good, and I will bring them again to this land; and I will build them up and not overthrow them, and I will plant them and not pluck them up And I will give them a heart to know Me for I am the Lord and they will be my people and I will be their God for they will return to Me with their whole heart'*

I did feel relieved and sure enough within a short time in late 2006 they returned to our hometown

They limped along, and in April 2007 as I was studying, God gently spoke to me He said,

> *"I'm going to bless Catherine and Tim today"*

I texted Catherine and told her what God had just told me! I wanted to encourage her. She texted back saying she was really sick. She was supposed to be starting a new job with Jaguar Cars but she was unable to start due to her being so ill. A week later it was confirmed that she was pregnant! I was worried for her and she began to tell me that the house they lived in was a high cost in rent and that she wanted to move. I helped her apply for council housing and she was offered a one bedroomed flat that was so deprived. There was mold on the walls and damp everywhere. I complained and she was eventually offered a house in another area. The house wasn't too bad and I was grateful after seeing the flat that at least she had this. Helping them move, both Hugh (yes, I missed Hugh, we started to see each other again) and I.

Just prior to Catherine's pregnancy announcement and just coming to the end of the first year of my degree, my lovely wonderful step- dad Jack died. He had suffered from Senile Dementia for about five years and was now at the end of his life.

One evening as Hugh and I left the hospital, I knew it would not be long before Dad would leave this world and go to be with Jesus in paradise. I was feeling quite low and to cheer me up Hugh asked if he could take me for meal at local pub. I agreed as I just wanted to go somewhere to escape the reality of what was about to happen with Dad. We found a place in the pub restaurant but I soon realised we had chosen the wrong place to sit. I wanted peace and to enjoy our meal chatting to each other. The large table next to us was rowdy with many of these diners merry with wine and laughing loudly. We asked to be moved to a quieter table and settled in for or meal. I had noticed a small table of two couples behind Hugh and as the night drew to a close, the woman from one of the couples, got up and went off to take the older couple home. The man was left on his own and I assumed the lady would come back for him once she has taken the other guests home. Hugh and I prepared to leave when I was suddenly prompted by the Lord,

"Invite the man over for coffee"

I stopped and sat back down again ushering Hugh to do the same. I said to him,

"Just wait God is speaking to me"

Again the same request. So I said to Hugh

"Ask that man to come and join us for a coffee?"

Hugh looked a bit pensive but agreed and turned in his chair to invite the man to come and join us"

The man declined his offer.

"I asked you to ask him" said the Lord.

I immediately called him over beckoning with my hand,

"Please come and join us for a quick coffee?"

The man got up and pulling a chair from a near table sat next to Hugh and me.

I began to tell him that I was a Cristian and that God had just told me to invite him to our table. His look did not betray his thoughts so I continued and told him my story, my testimony of how God drew me near to Him and lovingly brought me into the Kingdom.

The man listened intently, and I recall him placing his fingertips together from each hand and looking at them. Then he took a deep breath and spoke. He told us that he and his wife had been active members of the Christian Student Union in their university days and that he had been the head of this Student Union. However he said that something had happened and they had lost their faith in Jesus. He was now a dentist working with people who couldn't afford dental treatment. His wife then returned to the restaurant and was a little bemused to see her husband sitting with strangers having coffee and chatting. I explained to her the same conversation that I had with her husband and she too listened intently. Then it was time to leave. I don't know what happened to the couple, I just know that night God wanted to meet with them and in my grief, preparing for Dad to enter heaven, I was so open to touching heaven and felt the presence of the Lord all over this meeting with this man and his wife.

The next day as I sat by my Dad Jack in the hospital bed I read a word from the Lord which gave me great courage. Jack had been looking up to the corner of the ceiling in the hospital ward and pointing and waving. He smiled and said in wonder,

"Ooh hello" his eyes became bright as he waved a weary hand as if acknowledging someone. I looked up and seeing just the ceiling I asked him,

"Who can you see Jack?"

"They're all there; Joan, our Bill.....Oooh, can you hear that? It's beautiful, the angels are singing"

I was reading from the book of Philippians in the Bible. My eyes came to the last paragraph and it read:

'Now to our God and Father be the glory forever and ever Amen. Greet every saint in Christ Jesus. The Brethren that are with me greet you. All the saints greet you especially those of Caesar's household. The grace of our Lord Jesus Christ be with your Spirit'

I cried. It was as if the saints in the spirit were welcoming Jack home and he was getting ready to come. His feet were dry and his face was really dry too, so I used some aromatherapy oils to massage into his feet, I put the oils on his face and put salve on his lips. He looked peaceful and two days later he died.

I got the call just as I was starting my youth group session one Sunday evening at my work in Whitnash. Collecting my mum on the way through to the hospital, we arrived. The nurse told us he had just passed away and as I went in to see him still in the bed, mum was too upset and she stayed where she was in a waiting room.

As I prayed next to his body, which was still warm, I opened the Bible for a word, and my eyes alighted on the same scripture I read when Dad was alive! Only this time I felt I could hear my Dad saying,

"I'm with the saints now; I just wanted to let you know"

It's amazing how Father God can use His word and reveal by his Holy Spirit, the exact meaning He wants us to interpret.

John (JACK) Christopher O'Neill died 29th April 2007, my wonderful step-father.

And, as if to replace him, our beautiful, wonderful, grand -daughter Charley was born nine months later, to the day!

****

In June 2007, shortly after Dad's death, and still grieving in more ways than one, I decided that my relationship with Hugh was too much for me, yet again! So much was happening in my life and I wasn't sure he was the right man for me. To be honest, coping with the aftermath of Dad's death and getting through the first year of my degree was becoming too much for me to endure. I became poorly, breaking out in a rash that was caused by stress with a capital 'S'! I told Hugh I wanted to end our relationship as I felt it wasn't right for us to continue becoming more emotionally attached, especially with my doubts about being in a relationship at all! Hugh, being the gentleman he was and still is, received my rebuttal fairly well and we went our separate ways. I carried on studying hard and that summer I took up a part-time position as part of my course with Leamington Youth Offending Team. It seemed as though life was becoming easier. I volunteered to work on the evening food van which fed the local homeless in Leamington. I would take my little dog Zig out for long walks over the fields every day. I continued with my work and for a very long time, my life was a lot calmer. In the midst of a storm I had peace.

One day in mid- September 2007, Hugh's daughter had asked me if she could come and visit me for the day as she was over from Ireland. I knew her well as she had lived with Hugh while we were dating and I had become very fond of her. It was her 21st birthday the next day and she and Hugh were going over to Ireland for the arranged party. We had a lovely day together and I sent her off with a hug and a kiss.

The day after the party in Ireland, I was walking in the very early morning across the fields towards Bishop's Itchington. I stopped at a high point to look across the fields. The sun was just coming up on the horizon and there was a dull haze of morning mist hovering over the fields as far as the eye could see. It was quiet and it was as if the world was at a standstill. Very suddenly and without explanation, my heart began to ache for Hugh. I couldn't understand it! I hadn't seen him since late June and now all of sudden I wanted desperately to talk to him. I knew he had gone to Ireland for his daughter's 21st birthday party and I became concerned that he may stay and not come back to England. I sent him a text, right there and then, on the pretense that I wanted to know how the party went! But, he didn't return my text! I was distraught all day and had prematurely come to the conclusion that he was no longer interested in having a relationship with me. However late on the Saturday afternoon he called me. My heart leapt!

"I'm sorry I couldn't return your text straight away. I had run out of phone credits and there weren't any shops to buy any credit where we were staying!"

We talked for a long time. I was so happy to hear from him and I was immediately reminded of a word I had been given in late June by a mature Christian lady who had prayed for me regarding this relationship. She felt the Lord had given her a vision of a tree in blossom with bees gathering the nectar. She told me at the time she felt it wasn't the right season as yet, but fruit would soon appear. The next evening we arranged to meet up for the first time in three months and go for dinner. In fact, Hugh asked me to marry him and I said yes!!! After two years of deliberating over our relationship I had begun to see a man who was kind, loving, consistent, truthful, and full of integrity. Here was a strong faithful Christian man, he had wooed me with his gentle quiet love, never pushing me but allowing me like a butterfly to land on his heart when the time was right. I believe this timing was the anointing of the Lord. Hugh had returned back to God in full faith.

When I first met him he was angry with God, his faith had taken a battering but now here was a man back on track.

What a time! In the midst of my degree my Dad had died; my daughter was pregnant and needed my support, and I was about to get married.

CHAPTER 6

Bride and Groom- all comes together

The wedding preparations began. As I was in the midst of my studies, I knew the only possible time we could marry would be December when I had a Christmas break. Failing that, the following summer holidays. We didn't want to wait too long and decided we would try to marry in early December. Would it really be possible that my beloved 'Abbey' would be available at such short notice?

I cast my mind back to 1999. My late husband Stuart and I decided that when he came out of prison we would get married there and I had duly paid a deposit of £1000.00- a year in advance. Looking back, I realised that I'd subconsciously thought that if I paid the deposit it would definitely happen. I bought a beautiful gold wedding dress and was so excited. Of course our relationship fell apart and I managed to get the deposit back, but painfully I still had to pay for and fetch my dress from the wedding shop. I remembered going to pick up the dress on a cold, dreary January day. It was raining and miserable and that was just how I felt too. I had to pretend to the staff that we were soon to be married and I left the shop laden with dress, shoes, veil and crown; their voices of congratulations trailing out of the door with me as I kept a fixed grin upon my face, whilst deep inside, my heart was in tatters.

I drove to a private place and wept bitterly. How foolish I had been to believe I could ever have a relationship with Stuart. Just to push the dagger into my heart even further, a couple walked past the car hand in hand, and as if on cue, kissed each other with a tender embrace. I just wanted to be loved, that's all; I just wanted someone to show their love for me, to cherish me, to hold me. I so needed this right now and my whole being wrenched into desperation. I cried and howled like a baby. I was absolutely bereft. I told no one, only my dear friend Dee.

Now, here I was on the end of the telephone in late September 2007, enquiring about my beloved 'Abbey'. Did they have room for our wedding day early December?

"Can you accommodate a wedding on 1st or 8th of December please?" I said with some trepidation.

"Is it for 2008?" the receptionist asked.

"No, this year, 2007, please if it's possible?" I replied.

"This year? Well, I'll see what the diary looks like" she said in a defeated manner.

"I believe Lord", I prayed, *"that if we are to be married, you will have already set aside a space for us to be married on these dates"*

The lady came back to me.

"Well!" she said, with a manner of surprise and unbelief in her voice. *"There are no bookings at this time on the 1st of December in the large court which seats 100 guests or for the following week of 8th, we have the small room which seats 30 guests?"*

"Oh, that's great!" I was so delighted my heart leapt! *"Can we book the 1st December and the room which seats 100 guests please?"*

The lady seemed somewhat taken aback and as she wrote down my details she peppered them with inquisitive remarks.

"How lucky you got in! Has it been a quick decision?"

I laughed and said,

"Well, it's been coming for the past two years really we just needed to sort out the date" I said smiling from ear to ear.

That night as I was looking through my prayer journals I saw an entry I'd made in 2004, where I'd had a dream that I was getting married to a man in Leamington on a frosty day. Hugh also told me that a few years before he had been driving past St. Margaret's church, and had thought to himself,

"That would be a lovely church to get married in!"

Hugh and I married in early December at St Margaret's Church Whitnash where I was working and studying as a youth and community worker. The vicar was very gracious to allow my dear friend Simon another vicar to perform the actual wedding ceremony in the church. On the day of the wedding we were so blessed with friends who just opened their hearts and gave so generously of their love, time and gifting's. One of our lovely friends composed a wedding song and also taught our lovely group of young people from the youth group, to sing the songs he had composed; to worship and praise the Lord!

"This is the day the Lord has made we will rejoice and be glad"

All the young people I was walking alongside came to the wedding ceremony. The worship players included our dear friend Gary who played guitar and got the guests rocking in the aisles as they all waited for my appearance.

I was late as I wanted all my family to be there to witness my wedding day. They were not at my last two weddings and I wanted them to see how important my marriage to Hugh was.

Some of the young people were kind enough to actively help Hugh and me on the day. Nick and Tash were the ushers and the wonderful Peter as groomsman walked his lovely sister Nollie down the aisle as one of my official head bridesmaids. One of the youth leaders allowed us the use of a brand new white Jaguar range rover for the bridesmaids and our dear friend Simon drove us to the Abbey for our wonderful reception in a Vintage Jaguar. The late Charmaine Morris kindly read out a wonderful reading based on our Love for each other, she blessed us immensely. My dear friend Chris filmed the ceremony and the day for us. Michelle 'Gary's mighty woman of God' wife, gave us the most beautiful display of red roses surrounded by the deepest green ivy, and placed with huge cathedral candles into the vast spread of the arrangement. The whole contrast with the frosty winters' day and the gold of my dress with the colours of gold in Hugh's suit was exceptional. Everyone was so filled with joy it was a truly wonderful wonderful wonderful day!

Hugh and I decided to give everyone a glass candle holder with a candle inside with their name inscribed on the glass of each one and an individual scripture reference. Hugh asked me to give him some ideas for each person he didn't know, but I told him I was too busy and he should ask the Holy Spirit. He did and, my, oh my, the two bibles we brought in were being fought over at the wedding breakfast. One lady, whom neither of us really knew, was invited as she was staying with our good friends Robert and his wife Debs. When this woman read her scripture from the Bible, it really shook her and she demanded to know who had told us about her and her situation. Hugh explained nobody had told us anything; he had asked for guidance from the Holy Spirit and this was the scripture the Holy Spirit had told Hugh to give for this lady. She then demanded to know who the Holy Spirit was! This woman had been working with the darker things of this world and any spirit to her was certainly not the Holy Spirit.

John 16:12-15

'I still have many things to tell you, but you can't handle them now. But when the Friend comes, the Spirit of the Truth, he will take you by the hand and guide you into all the truth there is. He won't draw attention to himself, but will make sense out of what is about to happen and,

> *indeed, out of all that I have done and said. He will honour me; he will take from me and deliver it to you. Everything the Father has is also mine. That is why I've said, 'He takes from me and delivers to you'*

Who is the Holy Spirit?

For those readers who want a more defined answer of who the Holy Spirit is, I can tell you, that He is part of God. Together with God the Father and God the Son, there is God the Holy Spirit. He is the third person of this Trinity and makes up God who is community.

To explain this further man is created by God. The first of God's creation of man was Adam, then Eve was created from Adam's own bones. Together they had complete communion with God the FATHER. Only temptation came in the form of the serpent and he deceived them into tasting something of the forbidden from the tree of life. Once they had tasted of this fruit, their eyes became opened and they could see their nakedness and they had death and evil revealed to them. At this point they had discovered a dimension they were never meant to enter.

I sometimes see this as a young child suddenly experiencing evil that changes their life forever as an example in today's culture such as seeing things in the media that are evil, seeing or experiencing abuse. That child's life is affected by this event that the very evil act will define their lives forever, we too can allow ourselves to witness things we should not want to see. Many people traumatised by war, or death in a way that never leaves their minds.

When Adam and Eve had this revelation of evil revealed to them through their act of disobedience, their spirit within them died and was separated from their relationship with their creator. Time goes by and humanity is in darkness not knowing what was right or wrong. Moses chosen by God brought about the law- a set of rules, allowing hope to the people. It was through being given laws to abide by that man could start to understand what was right and what was wrong in the eyes of God their creator.

Let the reader understand that God as Father knew His people could not help but keep falling into temptation, doing wrong breaking these Commandments. At the right time He sent His only Son Jesus Christ- GOD HIMSELF IN THE FORM OF THE SON to restore life back to His people. When Jesus Christ died on the cross through the crucifixion, He paid our debt, the debt of man that had been disobedient and allowed the world –man, to experience sin and death. Jesus stood in the gap and died exchanging His life for ours. After three days DEATH could no longer hold Him and he rose again, the resurrection TIME. He went up to heaven AND JOINED His FATHER. In return the third person of God -The Holy Spirit was now enabled to come to us here on earth. He is here to restore us all back to God, we are given this revelation and knowledge of the truth of God that we are free to choose LIFE AND LIFE IN ALL ITS FULLNESS. We are INVITED to return to the wonderful presence of God for all time. All we need do is ask God to reveal Himself to us. Just as I did on that day back on my retreat in the caves, when I asked God,

"Are you real? Do you exist? Prove it to me" As soon as I asked for the truth of God with the true intent of trying to find the TRUTH, I gave permission for God to reveal Himself to me through Jesus Christ -because it was Jesus who redeemed us. The Holy Spirt was ignited in me and my spirit which was dead because of the first sin of Adam and Eve, was born again. It was not my old spirit being given life BUT the Spirit of God an essence of Him. My NEW SPIRIT within me is God himself coming to me and living in me. I am a NEW CREATION. The old has gone. I now have a relationship back with my heavenly Father through the saving grace of Jesus Christ and the Holy Spirit is here now while I live on this earth in my human body to lead me and guide me out of my old ways, to grow in maturity into the true person, the true identity God created me to be. No longer a slave to sin and death but free to live and work to Gods praise and glory. And as with any new relationship, we need time to invest ourselves in God our Father getting to know Him by living daily by coming into His presence. We do this by intentionally reading His word, singing to Him, praying to Him, talking to Him. It is the Holy Spirt of God here on earth to help us, to comfort us, to guide and lead us into all the truth of God. We have been given Him as a gift from God, to be with us on earth. This means we can talk to Him. We can ask questions and He will answer them for us. As you see from my story He has shown up in all sorts of situations I've been in, to guide me and show me His deep Love for me and for others. People can fall into the trap of getting too busy doing 'Good works', but this is a false deception. We MUST put our eyes on God, and as Sister Maria (you'll meet her later in the book) my wonderful spiritual director, said

"Look adoringly at Jesus"

Once we understand the deep love and joy He is granting to us we can then go and work in the field as it were to allow others to come to know that they too can be given this new Spirit of love if they ask for it. Just as I did. If you compare the first part of my book the old story to the new story in this latter part of the book you will understand that I am a completely new person in God. I am free alive and enjoying my new life in Kingdom living here in earth- Yes heaven starts when you say YES to Jesus my friend!

Hugh and I started married life together. My study continued as Hugh worked. In January 2008 the Lord blessed us all with a beautiful granddaughter, Charley. I was there at her birth and as I held her after the delivery into this world, I gave thanks to our God and blessed her all the days of her life.

CHAPTER 7

The next up-grade

In 2009 I graduated from University with a very respectable 2:1 Bachelor of Arts with Honours in the field of Youth & Community and Applied Theology. I say it with pride as it was a huge achievement after three years of stress and strain as I explained earlier in my book.

When on course with the agenda that God has set for us, it seems that everything falls into place regarding all the details. We felt the promptings of the Holy Spirit, especially during the final six months of my course. I began to feel that the Lord was moving us on. I began to look for posts in the field of youth and community work. And we also bought a diesel car as I felt we would be going quite far from Leamington Spa.

As if to position ourselves we began to get our home ready for the rental market. I applied and got a new post in the New Forest area, we had to rent to begin with. Just as we were leaving a friend from a Church Organisation told us a new intern was going to be living in Whitnash and at the same time the tenant for our first home in the New Forest, was also leaving. As usual God was ahead of us and we managed to prepare our home for rental and leave, with the new intern moving in the same week we moved out and we in turn moved into our new home as the old tenant left that week too.

I applied for a post as the new Youth & Community Pastor at a church in the New Forest and was successful. Hugh gave notice in his employment and we left Leamington Spa with excitement and trepidation!

Charley our little granddaughter was two years old at the time. I was worried about leaving Catherine, Tim and Charley. We were very much part of all their lives and to leave was a real sacrifice because I knew I was really leaving them in God's hands. But when God calls you, He promises if we are faithful to Him, He is faithful to us. I comforted myself with the fact that we would only be living about two hours away by car, so could back fairly quickly if need be.

It wasn't long before the old enemy of rejection and betrayal reared its ugly head. The work I began to do was very much anointed. There were many people who loved us and supported the work. I had volunteers and met some great people to work alongside. I created a team and we worked with young people in the village who had little connection or no connection with Jesus.

The 'Drop- In' was created and held in our youth centre. It attracted young people just on the edge of their mid-teens. Throughout the banter and swearing and sometimes disruptive behaviour, Hugh and I and others from our church and community began to show up, showing love and consistency. Relationships were developing. We walked alongside them. This was going well and I began to see that Monday evenings (a time when the centre was available) would be a great time to get the group together and reflect on a deeper understanding of who Jesus was for them, as well as for us. I envisioned this would begin by the time the third and final year of my contract was starting. Little did I realise I was due an up- grade in my true identity with God and my plans began to change direction.

My work was great, although, I had come to realise that there were two different thought streams from others as to my job specification, which included two different churches vying for position for their youth work. I was caught up in the middle and the back lash for me was that I began to feel the pressure of not being able to please both. The pressure came with criticism, lies, rejection and hurtful gossip.

I sought solace one day in the quiet of the nearby beautiful priory; a small order of 'sisters' who reside and work within this restful place. I took along my friend and prayer partner Pauline. We decided to go into the chapel and seek the silence so that we could listen to what the Lord wanted to share with us. As we were sitting there, I reflected back to my first visit to this lovely chapel when I initially arrived to take up my new post. A small group of us had come to spend a few hours in the chapel, to pray and hear from God. Over that next hour we were entertained by a mighty weather storm which just appeared unexpectedly! There was a violent wind with torrential rain, followed by strikes of lightening. The horses in the nearby fields were high-tailing like crazy around the surrounding fields. We were alone in the chapel; nobody else came in until the time we left. As we prayed, nobody spoke. We just looked out of the window at this magnificent display of God's power. At the end of the hour we were all incredulous as to the meaning of such a torrential storm. Someone even joked and said,

"I bet the sisters wonder who is in the chapel and what we were praying for!" We all laughed.

On this occasion, Pauline and I stepped into the chapel as the sisters were delivering their mid-morning service. It was lovely as we stepped in, to be greeted by beautiful smiling faces and we immediately felt that we were allowed to be there. We listened as the sisters sang through some of the service with songs and psalms. As we left one of the sisters approached us in the foyer. She asked where we had come from and I introduced myself, as did Pauline. I told her I was the new youth pastor in the nearby church. She was delighted to meet us and had said the sisters had heard I had come. She said they prayed for the young people every day at 11 am. She told me her name was Sister Mary. I suddenly felt a jolt in my spirit and I told her,

"I am looking for a spiritual support to help me step out of my situation and help me to hear what God is saying to me?"

Sister Mary was very welcoming and smiled so lovingly at me. I knew she really cared for me and my situation. I went to visit her once or twice a month and she spiritually guided me through the rocky road I was currently walking on. We delved into books she suggested and my spirit drank in the enormous wealth of her Godly wisdom and love. Once, near Christmas time, I went on my regular visit and after we had our meeting Sister Mary suggested I go into the chapel and spend some time looking at the nativity display. She explained that to look adoringly at Jesus is all we need to do and the rest will fall into place. I must admit, it was another three years before that penny dropped and I began to really understand that I needed to put Jesus first; to love Him, seek Him in all things pertaining to my life; to press into knowing Him more and more, whether through trials and tribulation, or peace and stillness.

But at this time, as I began to struggle with what I perceived as betrayal and rejection, I became stressed and sick. My upgrade was proving tough. I was not only dealing with the stressful times at work, but my concerns for my family were also making me fearful. I just couldn't seem to find the peace I so longed for. There were times, however, when I would be delighted in what God was doing through the work and the young people.

One day one of the young lads came to see me. He was extremely distressed. After a long chat, I began to understand that he had been involved in something quite demonic and evil. I won't go into detail, suffice to say, this young man was very frightened and told me he had nowhere to turn; that he would have to die to protect himself and his family. I told him that there was hope! The hope of Jesus Christ. I told him that when we believe, by faith, in Jesus Christ, He will come and protect us and show us the right pathway out of any situation and He brings about the opportunity for those pathways to open. What seems so hopeless in our lives is full of potential for God and He truly loves to reveal His power over our hopeless situations, literally kicking Satan up the back side and right out of our lives. Then, when He rescues us, He surrounds us with the right people, who cherish and love us back to health. This young man, after asking many questions, made a life changing decision. He prayed, he thanked Jesus for dying on the Cross for him; he said sorry for the ways he had been sinful in his life and finally, he asked Jesus to be the Lord over his life in the future; to guide him and lead him on that right pathway away from darkness and evil. He gave his life to Jesus, firmly trusting that Jesus was able to sort this mess out that he found himself in.

Unfortunately, my plans to teach the village young people more about 'hope' were dashed when I decided I couldn't take any more stress. I gave up *my* hope and I quit my post. I was too hurt and could not continue the way matters were. It all came down to expectations. People with influence getting their own agendas, commanding their way as opposed to the expectation of the role I was given by the church as a whole. God was leading my heart in one way as others who had their own interest as opposed to Kingdom interests were pulling me the other way. I had worked to build up trust and love with the village young people who had known nothing of Jesus and I was about to embark on a deeper connected group with them as my third year kicked in, only satan got in. God had placed every resource at my disposal to come through with this little group of teenagers, but I was not strong enough to deliver His will. The wounds of betrayal and rejection from others cut deep. God in this time I realise was revealing not only the state of my heart but of those involved. I can't say for them what they learned from this situation and hurtful time, but I was able to grow so much from this experience.

One thing I realise is that regardless of what we do, who we do it for and why; we are here on the earth for God's pleasure. I don't mean he can mess about and make us miserable and then make us alright again. God is 'Love' and from the day we were born he has been calling us back to be with Him, not just when we go to heaven but to experience all of His love while we are still in our human form on the earth. He knows we want to feel validated, loved and accepted, because that's our true identity that God has created us to be. It's a given fact that we want to be who we truly are. So when I felt betrayal and rejection from my situation, God was allowing me an opportunity to inspect this area of my life where I just didn't feel 'good enough'; where I just felt useless; where I just felt the painful stab of betrayal. Lies and accusations secretly put against me, not for the whole church to hear just the group who wanted 'THEIR' way. (Please let the reader understand that I could go into the details of this, but I am now healed from this situation and have truly forgiven and love these people.) What was happening was that God was saying,

"Stop looking at them, look at me!"

What did that mean? I didn't know. I couldn't figure it out. Then one day, when I felt really low, God gave me the vision of a bird. I had to die to self. My own ego wanted to be recognised as a great person; not someone who was an outsider that felt unwelcome. The upgrade took me another two years to receive. It was already there, I just didn't know how to get it!

The Holy Spirit guided me, firstly through the circumstances that I had left the village in, leaving behind all the young people, children and families I had worked and lived with. People whose lives God had impacted through my work as they impacted my life too. The beauty of the New Forest a place of outstanding beauty with its deep forests and walkways both integrally wound around beautiful olde worlde villages steeped in history, with the adaption into the nearby trendy seaside villages with their boats and yachts moored into the shore line.

The cottage where we had lived was on the actual forest -over the cattle grids, allowing horses and donkeys as well as pigs and cattle to roam freely in the vast area of this scenic beauty. The cottage so adorably English with roses around the door and the quaint cottage interior of thick white washed walls and quaint little windows that looked out onto the donkeys and horses which trotted past on their way to another feeding time somewhere on the forest. The smell of wood burning fires in the late autumn and winter evenings whilst the darkest of nights allowed the glistening of a multitude of stars in heavens best show.

On leaving this beautiful place, Sister Mary handed me a picture of Mary and Joseph escaping to Egypt away from Herod with the baby Jesus; refugees in a land that wasn't their own. Then she led me to the story of the Israelites who left Egypt with Moses. She said my leaving was like that time, when the Israelites left Egypt for the Promised Land. She asked me a pertinent question,

"What did God ask them to do before they left?"

It was to plunder their Egyptian neighbours for their gold and silver. Sister Mary said to me,

"Take the gold and silver of your experiences here and use them when you reach the Promised Land"

How wise she was! I was able to take those experiences of my time in the forest and use them to reveal the next step; the REVELATION of looking at and ADORING, Jesus; not looking at myself. I began to understand that to truly be accepted and loved, I FIRST HAVE TO LOVE JESUS AND LOVE MYSELF THROUGH KNOWING I AM LOVED BY HIM, otherwise my capacity to love is limited to the way and the level I love myself.

When I was in the New Forest, my defense was to verbally hit back to defend my ground. I began to understand that Jesus never justified himself. There is power in that! I realised to break through the hurts of rejection and betrayal was by asking God to change me. I stopped asking God to change others. Their lives were none of my business and, instead of judgement, I just blessed them with God's love. It wasn't easy at first and I admit at times even now, there are certain people I really wouldn't care to see again in my life, but I'm in a process and, I'm willing to be completely healed from that hurt. I continue to bless them, when I remember!

I now experience more of God's love. I continually ask Him to change me to love those who will probably never love or accept me, but as I said that's not for me to be concerned about. My concern is how much love I can get from God. The gold and silver experiences allowed me to assess and understand the path back to acceptance. I can readily receive from God,

"Change Me! Change Me! Change Me!" I say to the Lord. It's so liberating!

Hugh and I stayed a further six months in the area, being nurtured and nourished by some lovely people who are still great friends to this day. We continued our work with the village kids in the youth centre which allowed me to give them the closure they needed, through giving information of our departure in the summer months. I didn't want them to feel rejected, so it was important to end our relationships properly to show our love and respect to them, which I believe we did. We prepared to leave by the summer of 2012.When we did leave it was a calling back to our home town and our lovely family to help take care of our daughter, our granddaughter and family.

CHAPTER 8

Pressing into God

As January 2012 rolled in, we were still living in the New Forest. I was without work and no longer receiving the salary we had been relying on to carry us through to the end of the following summer. We still had a commitment to pay bills which now seemed impossible as my wages would now be at a significant loss. I was also looking at the prospect of supporting my daughter Catherine. It seemed that everything was conspiring against me and Hugh as we battled through this tough season. Catherine knew that the school years for Charley would be upon us soon and she would have to ensure Charley had this support. Tim was struggling to take care of the family and so it was decided that they would come and stay with us for time. Tim would stay at home.

I have to acknowledge my husband Hugh, who with the help of the Lord God, carried me through this darkest time. I thank him from the bottom of my heart and soul for his consistent love and devotion to me and my family.

Catherine was weak and came back to the New Forest to live with us. The strain was tremendous as we tried to make ends meet. Hugh was working full time and also helping me to look after our little granddaughter and Catherine. We managed to get Charley into a little nursery which gave me a break as I was beginning to feel quite ill. One day I became quite sick; I was having tremendous pain in my stomach, so much so, I ended up in hospital. It was very scary as I had not stayed in hospital since the birth of my daughters, so this was not easy for me. Hugh looked after Charley and Catherine and worked full time too! We were blessed with good friends who helped us through.

As I lay in my hospital bed I began to reflect on all that was going on and asked God to reveal to me what I needed to do. I remember that the weekend I was admitted, the hospital was on an emergency code as it was full to capacity. I had been sitting on a chair, enduring immense pain, whilst waiting to be seen. I prayed and shortly I was taken by wheelchair to have an X-ray. As I waited in the corridor the pain became so excruciating I could not sit there and I writhed in agony on the floor. Two porters caught hold of me as I sobbed with the pain. They were very kind and I could see they were upset for me. As soon as the X-ray was done they whisked me up to a ward and wheeled the trolley into a bed space. I was promptly given tablets as the pain was too much. As the sweat trickled down my back I thought I was dying. The tablets worked quickly and soon I was in a state of calm. The doctor was not sure what was wrong with me and decided to keep me in for tests.

I recall that even though I was not happy to be there, it was a break from the trauma and as I began to rest I suddenly began to make time to ask God what I was doing there.

While I was there, the Lord was able to put some very special people in my path and I was able to tell them about the Lord Jesus. I was placed in a six bed ward alongside a lovely lady called Eileen. As we chatted throughout the day, I began to tell her about my story; my walk with Jesus. I told her my testimony. As she listened, I noticed the other ladies in the ward were listening too. That day Eileen asked Jesus into her life. While writing this book (some two years later) I decided that I would call her and see if she was still with us. (When I met Eileen she had just been diagnosed with cancer). I called her phone number and ended up having a wonderful conversation with Eileen's husband. She had sadly died a year after our meeting. I am so glad I was able to be open to the 'God incidence' of meeting such a wonderful woman and knowing that through our conversation and her commitment to follow Jesus she is now in paradise with Him. Her husband chatted with me for a long time and I was able to tell him about Jesus. He was very cautious and said he would rather believe 'what will be, will be'. I know that God loves him and will send another person as a sign post to him.

Remarkably the doctor could not discover any problems and my pain left me, never to return and off I went home, stepping back into the melee of my own life.

In late April 2012 Catherine decided to return home with Charley she was feeling stronger and healthier. We went to visit them in early May. We helped decorate Charley's room. Tim and Hugh did most of the work, we had a good day and on our return to the New Forest it was then that the lord broke in and spoke to me. Hugh was driving and I suddenly felt the Lord say,

"It's time to return"

I suddenly looked at Hugh; my heart was beating fast. What would this mean? Hugh would have to hand in his notice at work; we would have to leave our lovely cottage and we would have to give notice to our tenant renting our house in Leamington Spa! We would be saying goodbye to some wonderful friends and a lovely lifestyle of sun and sea!

"Darling?" I said to Hugh,

"I just got a sense that God is calling us back to home. How do you feel about that?"

Hugh smiled at me and said,

"The Lord has told me the same thing; I was waiting for you to confirm it!"

We smiled and as we continued on the journey down the A34, right there in front of us, was the most amazing rainbow..........we smiled!

We were going to go home!

Our planned return went well under the circumstances. I want to acknowledge our dear friends Sue and Jo who stood with us through all our challenges and became the solid rocks we could rely on and trust and my heart will love you both forever.

When we arrived back in Leamington Spa, it was June 28th 2012, the day before my 49th birthday.

On the day Hugh and I arrived back, Catherine called us and asked us to pick up Charley.

Catherine's health had taken a turn and she was just too weak to look after her all the time, and she was also now on her own as Tim had left.

We were back in our own home in Leamington, thankfully there wasn't a mortgage on the house and so we did not have to pay rent, but suddenly, here we were with no jobs to go to. We had no money so we both decided we would need to claim benefits. Hugh had never claimed benefits and I had not claimed since I was a teenager. We applied online and this took nearly two hours. We then had to wait for a meeting with the benefits agency. In the meantime, our good friend Claire loaned us £500. We had bills to pay and I was dreadfully worried and felt scared and depressed.

I remembered Gods promise to me in Isaiah 43:2

> *'When through the deep waters I call thee to go, the rivers of sorrow shall not overflow. For I will be with thee, thy troubles to bless and sanctify thee thy deepest distress'*

We helped Catherine get Charley into a new school for September. We immediately put the Leamington house up for sale. In hindsight (which is a great thing!), we thought that as we had no money, we needed to sell the house and buy a place near Catherine. In the meantime, as we waited for it to be sold we had no jobs, no money and, the loan from our friend was gone. I, more so than Hugh, felt ashamed that we had suddenly come to a place where for the first time in a very long time we had no money for food. We prayed and I told Hugh I didn't want us to borrow any more money. My pride could no longer take the shame I was feeling. We had been battered by events and circumstances over the past six months and I could no longer cope with trying to explain and tell people about our predicament; it was all too much. We were tired and drained and were battle weary. We attended our chosen church that was also the church that had been trying to support Catherine. We were supported there. We did not tell anyone about the crisis we were going through. I just sobbed throughout the worship time allowing God to minister to me and return some peace to me.

As we waited for our benefits to be sorted, we needed to apply for an emergency loan as we had no money at all. Charley was attending a nursery in the week and we didn't want her life to change as she loved her nursery. We wanted to support Catherine so we would travel to Catherine's to fetch Charley and take her to nursery.

We applied for the emergency fund which took three hours of telephone calls to set up. Suddenly we were told to come and get the money from the benefits office, fifteen miles away in Stratford on Avon. We thanked God for this much needed provision at that time.

We both felt trapped and it seemed to us that God was not around. I felt so miserable and depressed, but we had to keep going. Silly problems seemed to happen, for instance, I applied for jobs in one week instead of spreading it over two weeks and my benefit was stopped so I didn't receive any financial help for those two weeks. I was angry and upset.

Our breakthrough came when I was told of a family support worker job that was opening up from September for the right candidate. I decided this was exactly the right work for me and applied for the post.

At the same time we sold the house and the sale was due to be completed by mid-August 2012.

My friend Angie told us she wanted to move from her house, as it was too big for her, and get a smaller place. We decided we would rent the house with a proviso that we would possibly end up buying it the following year once we got settled and Hugh was working too. After a stringent interview I was offered the post as family support worker with a large local school.

I began my post as Charley began school. We were really happy that we were able to support our family, and Hugh was able to take Charley to school when Catherine needed our help. Hugh was able to take her and pick her up.

We now, finally, had the money from our house sale in the bank and we felt quite secure. We had moved into my friend's house and she moved out to a new home.

I began my role as a family support worker and the Lord just anointed the work I did. I was on a steep learning curve and I appreciated that. No longer was I to drink the milk of babes, but eat the meat of a mature Christian and I knew I was still in the deep waters.

One day, I came into my little quiet office on the third floor of the school. The internet connection was down and basically I couldn't do my work as I needed to work online. It seemed all my plans were frustrated. Suddenly I thought to myself,

"Lord, I'm just going to give this time to you, I can't do my work so you must want me to draw near to you."

I pulled out my Charles Spurgeon devotional book and began to read. Within a minute the telephone rang. It was one of my parents who I supported; I'll refer to her as Wendy. She told me her son had refused to come to school as he needed some paracetamol for a painful foot. I told her I had these tablets and would come and fetch him and bring him to school. When I arrived at the house I realised Wendy was very sick, her breathing was laboured and she could hardly speak. I told her I was calling an ambulance. I'm sorry to say the ambulance was not forthcoming and after another call, an ambulance finally arrived. Into the house arrived two paramedics who were two young women. As Wendy laboured for breath the one paramedic, who seemed to be the boss, said that her breathing was fine. As Wendy began to deteriorate I noticed the two girls look at each other and a smirk crossed their faces, as if to say

"What a drama Queen!"

I was not happy. It crossed my mind if Wendy was living in a higher priced house in a more select area of the city, she may have been treated differently.

"I don't know what you find so amusing young lady?" I said to the one I perceived as the leader, *"If I were you I would be very concerned as I can see her condition deteriorate in the last ten minutes. I would think about getting her to hospital quickly".* I said this in a firm voice with my eyes holding her gaze.

The paramedic dropped her smile and considered my words for a brief moment.

Without saying another word she began to listen to Wendy's breathing.

"It does seem that her breath going in is fine but there is an obstruction as she breathes out"

I could feel this paramedic's pride take the better of her. She knew there was a problem and now she was going to look foolish in front of her younger colleague. As if to mitigate her prideful hurt, she said,

"She will be able to walk to the ambulance" and with that the two paramedics helped her up.

Wendy was shaken and unstable.

"I'm sure it would have been better to carry her into the ambulance" I remarked.

The paramedic avoided my eyes and said,

"We're almost in now". She wasn't going to break her pride to give in and allow Wendy to be carried on a stretcher.

I didn't push it but tried to comfort Wendy who was worried about who would look after her three children when they got home from school.

I told her not to worry and that it was all in hand and I would make sure they were cared for.

Her eldest son was worried and he went in the ambulance with his mum as I went off in search of the social care team who were supporting the family. They were all in meetings with no one available. I sat in my car and thought for a moment.

"Lord what shall I do for this family right now?" My mind cast back to the previous week. Wendy had been having issues with benefits and was without food. I was able to get her a food voucher and as she was so low and depressed and not wanting to leave the house, I went and fetched the food on their behalf. There was a major abundance of food that week, from huge cakes and fresh meat and vegetables to all the staple food required. Right in the middle of the box was a packet of square crisps. When I had arrived at the house Wendy's youngest son was very eager to help me put the shopping away. When he caught sight of the packet of square crisps he squealed with delight,

"Look Mum" he said, *"There's a packet of square crisps, can I have them please?"*

Wendy had smiled and said that he could have them.

As if to qualify for the crisps he said,

"You sit there mum and I'll put all the food away so you can rest."

He put out his hand in a 'Stop, don't move' action, to his mum; this angelic little eight year old with blonde hair was choosing to be the man of the house today.

This little incident touched my heart and it ached. As I drove off from their home that day, the Lord gently answered a question I'd asked Him about a week previous. I had been thinking about the day I had first heard His voice in that church in Rottendean. In the song it said,

"I will hold your people in my heart." I had asked God recently to explain how I was going to hold His people in my heart?

And now as small tears trickled down my cheek after being so touched by this little boy and his mummy, I heard the Lord say,

"This is how you hold My people in your heart" I felt the Lord gently look at me with a loving smile. I broke down and wept. I was doing what He had called me to do from the day I heard Him and recognised His voice.

And now these people were tightly being held in my heart as I began to seek God's advice on what I should do. Going back to the office, I contacted the younger boy's school and told them his mummy was in hospital. They contacted a close friend of Wendy's who said she would pick him up and take care of him till mummy was home. I then decided to go to the hospital and find out how Wendy was doing. When I arrived I was shocked to see her condition. She was on an oxygen ventilator and was clearly struggling. In between breaths, she told me she was worried about her children. The hospital had said she would not be going home that day; she was too sick. I told her I would go and sort out the arrangements and come back and tell her. I fetched her daughter from our school that was able to identify an aunt she wanted to stay with. Having met and chatted with the aunt, I left the daughter there and arranged for the friend to have the youngest son overnight. The oldest boy was allowed an older cousin to come and stay. After supplying him with food for a few days, I went back to the hospital. Wendy had been diagnosed with clots on her lungs and was lucky to be alive! I prayed with her and she was grateful. We had, over time, been talking about God and I told Wendy about Jesus. When

Wendy came out of the hospital I told her much more about Jesus; she had also been attending an Alpha course at the local Baptist church. I am thrilled to say that today Wendy is an active member of her church, is baptised and is growing in the Lord.

The work I was doing was so good, yet sadly I was having to do more and more paper work to conform to the educational procedures and policies on safe guarding and all that comes with the territory and I was spending less and less time with people. I decided to leave.

I felt a sense of failure. I had been doing such a great work; did I sabotage my own success? Was I being too choosy? It didn't feel great to leave as I was just settling in and in hind sight I should have stayed a while longer. The old doubts about my old post in the New Forest came flooding in and I felt like a failure and I felt shame. This was not good.

The money in the bank was worrying me. We both needed to work yet we had to take time for our little granddaughter. How could we do this? I had a sense that if I were to gain employment elsewhere, with another organisation, it would take charge over my life and unless I truly trusted the organisation, how would I be able to live for another's expectations whilst feeling I wanted to work for God.

Hugh and I decided that we would look to buy into a business of some kind. We had always wanted some kind of business and I had dreams of being my own boss. I would be able to have people work for me and I could fetch Charley from school and if she was ill we could take time off and look after her. We would be able to afford lovely holidays and all in the garden would be rosy!

We looked at a beauty business primarily and there was a beautiful place in a very select surrounding village. However, after examining the books we realised this business was not viable.

I then found out about a beautiful restaurant for sale, in Warwick town centre and after perusing, what we thought, were the legitimate, financial accounts, it seemed that this business could be a real winner for us.

It was a seventy seater restaurant, in a small cobbled street in Warwick town centre. Using the money from the house sale we began to the process of stepping into the world of business.

We secured the lease and set about restoring, buying equipment and gathering staff. Within two months we were up and running. It was now July 2013.

Just around this time, my daughter Catherine was beginning to feel better, we had been praying for her healing and now there was a breakthrough. She started to become brighter and alert; she even became the manageress of our restaurant. She did an excellent job!

I remembered though, all the promises that God gave me for Catherine and I thanked Him that He had indeed restored her back to health.

There are times in my life when I want to believe that I am really hearing from God and that He will bless everything I do. The blessings do come! However, as the example of our buying the restaurant reveals, it does not always come in the way we want or expect it to.

I had personally prayed for the restaurant business to be a success. I told God we would use our profits to bless others. Surely I thought, what we were doing would honour God so much He would bless us in the business even more?

Unfortunately, the restaurant was losing profits from day one. The deeper we went to try to make it a success, the deeper the debt got. Hugh and I worked so hard and we faced many new battles. During this time the stresses overwhelmed us and we began to bicker with one another. We also had to work on either end of the day. One of us working in the morning, one of us taking over to cover the evening. So we never really spent any quality time together. By November, I hated going there. As we worked on the figures and the marketing strategies we just felt like we were flogging a dead horse, so to speak. My quiet time with the Lord was almost non-existent, as was my quality time with Hugh and our family.

"Why are we in this mess?" I cried out to the Lord, as if I didn't know!

His silence was not good, as I continually baited Him for an answer. One day, I felt like I'd lost my faith! I felt I had made some terrible mistake by wasting the money He had provided for us on this business. I was ashamed and, worse still, I felt quite hopeless. I started to pray in earnest, begging God to forgive me. I had gone my own way to pursue money and self-seeking success. I wanted to be the owner of an exclusive restaurant that people would come running to. Don't misunderstand me; God *will* give you the desire of your heart; He isn't a mean God! But now, I know, as well as believe, that desire comes from Him. I also know that my ultimate desire, is to be the person God has truly created me to be in this world, and I now realise that the pursuit of fame and money through the restaurant was a complete distraction, opened up to us after our sense of failure from our time in the New Forest. We had fallen for the old, dangling carrot and I believe we thought we needed to prove ourselves in man's eyes. Now, we were about to face the consequences. We were in another 'upgrade' spiritually and I knew it wasn't going to be too pleasant. The Lord began to reveal my heart to me, and I can tell you I was not impressed with that!

I realised I had issues with people who seemed to live a life of material richness, without having a care in the world about others who struggle; families in poverty for example.

I cast my mind back to my time in the New Forest. I remembered on one particular day I took a walk along the sea front and deciding to sit in the shelters provided, I watched the sea as it ebbed and flowed with the sun making diamond twinkling patterns on the waves. It was glorious. As if by some God-incidence, an old man rode up to the shelter and placed his bicycle against the wall. Smiling at me as he sat down, we both greeted one another. We passed comment on the sunshine and the prevailing wind; it was all very pleasant. I then asked God a question,

"Lord, what do you want me to say to this man?" As I recall, I realised I was walking later than I usually did and suddenly I realised I had been pottering around the house as if I was subconsciously waiting for the timing to be right to go on the walk! I asked the man where he was from.

He told me he was from London and that he had recently retired and moved to the New Forest vicinity. He had been a printer by trade. He asked me about my work and I told him that I was the youth pastor for a local church. I also told him about my work with young people with addiction issues.

The man then told me, that when he was in business, he had 'people like that' who came to drop off paper at the printers where he had worked and also pick up parcels. They were volunteering and he said he never wanted anything to do with them; so his staff dealt with them!

"I work with these people to support them to get out of their addiction and to know who Jesus Christ is". I was testing the waters and this man looked astounded and totally surprised.

"Why would you do that?" he said.

I looked into this man's eyes.

"Do you have a faith?" I asked him.

"My parents were Jewish, as am I and my family, but I don't practice anything" he said.

"I am a Christian" I said, and I told him a brief summary of my walk so far with God. I suddenly felt the need to ask the question *"Where do you think we go when we die?"* I turned to ask him.

"I don't believe we go anywhere" He replied, *"I've had a good life, earned good money, my sons will inherit it and when I'm gone that's it, there's nothing more."*

I looked him straight in the eye and said this,

"I believe that we have eternal life set up for us in heaven, Jesus said, "For God so loved the world that he gave His only begotten Son, that whoever believes in Him will not perish, but have eternal life."

There, the Holy Spirit had opened the man's mind to His truth. There was no way it was ever going to be forgotten this man had been given the word, now planted in his mind for a time until God was to reveal more of Himself to the man.

The man looked angry, he suddenly said,

"I have to go now," and with that he got on his bicycle and rode off.

"Good bye", I said *"it was lovely talking to you, bless you!"*

I knew that the meeting had been a divine, set time and I quietly thanked God and prayed that He would continue to reveal His love to this man.

The point I wanted to make was that this man, who by his own admission had lived a good life, was completely unaware of a life after death. He also seemed to be angry with people with addictions whom he said he didn't want to deal with. God makes it very clear in His word that there will be people who will be so blinded by the god of this world that they will not see and understand the gospel of Jesus and the salvation and freedom they can walk in.

In 2 Corinthians 4:3-4 Paul the apostle tells us,

> [3] *But even if our Gospel (the glad tidings) also be hidden (obscured and covered up with a veil that hinders the knowledge of God), it is hidden [only] to those who are perishing and obscured [only] to those who are spiritually dying and veiled [only] to those who are lost.*

> *[4] For the god of this world has blinded the unbelievers' minds [that they should not discern the truth], preventing them from seeing the illuminating light of the Gospel of the glory of Christ (the Messiah), Who is the Image and Likeness of God.*

I realised that a part of me wanting to be successful financially was to show certain people that we were successful too and not failures, as I had previously felt after the betrayal and rejection in my work at in the New Forest. I was shocked that even after two years of leaving that position, I was still making choices based on my sense of failure. I was still allowing the choices made by others to affect my life! And the worst thing is, that God had allowed us to go ahead and throw away the only money we had! Now here we were, Hugh and I, questioning, at different times, our dilemma and our faith in God.

One day in early November I cried out to God,

"Lord, I am so sorry for going my own way, please forgive me!" I cried tears streaming down my face. *"Lord, if there is a way out of this restaurant business please show us! Please?"* The answer came immediately.

"Close it"

"Close it, Lord?? What about all our customers who have booked for Christmas day; who have paid deposits?"

Nothing. Just silence.

As if bartering with God, I said *"Ok Lord, I'm going to close it after business on Christmas Day".*

Hugh was in full agreement. We couldn't continue as we were and we could limp on till Christmas Day to fulfil our obligations to the customers who had booked and paid deposits.

From that time, I felt a sense of relief and I was able to return to a quiet place with God; praying; reading His word and fellowshipping with our church family even more. Hugh on the other hand, was going through his own spiritual crisis. In fact, he woke up one morning and stared at the ceiling. I could tell he was upset.

After a time he said,

"I'm not sure about this God thing anymore. If there is a God, I think He's having a bit of laugh. Not just at me, but my whole family".

I can understand how he felt, when we get to the lowest toughest times in our lives we can be feeling so low that we are suddenly bombarded with untruths that begin to take hold and then our imaginings begin to take hold and we see the worst case scenario.

In a recent talk given by Pastor Martin Storey from CLM Church Coventry he spoke on the theme of 'Your Tomorrow is Coming' using the story of how the king of Israel whose life was under siege- read it for yourself in 2 Kings 6:24-7:20.

The talk was based on how we as human beings can lose our perspective and priority when 'under siege'. We begin to value things wrongly, we can get caught up in other people's dramas as if we have to solve those, while dealing with our own siege. We can also begin to blame others for the mess.

We are guided by God very clearly to hold our ground, to stand firm on the promises of God and begin to position ourselves to hear from Him. We need to step out in faith as if our promise from God will be here tomorrow.

It was true that all our immediate family seemed to be under siege and I would say things were not looking good for us at all.

I called one of Hugh's brothers, Alex and asked him over to our home. He is a wonderful man of God in many ways. I was concerned about this whole situation and felt the urgency of going to the prayer room. This was a time we needed to step out in faith, we had begun to lose our perspective and we had been playing the blame game with each other. Now was the time to stop and with faith position ourselves before the Lord to hear from Him and be encouraged that this whole situation was not our future, and our tomorrows were certainly on their way.

The next day Hugh, his brother, and I, began an intense time of worship and praise before the Lord. As we worshipped, we petitioned God for the McNeill family. We prayed in earnest for our deliverance and to have the strength to overcome in this challenging season of our lives. We began to cry out loud to the Lord declaring His promises to rescue us; I felt directed to read out loud Psalm 18 and so began to proclaim these promises from God our Father, and as I did, an amazing thing happened!

Psalm 18

1 I love you, LORD, my strength.

2 The LORD is my rock, my fortress and my deliverer;
my God is my rock, in whom I take refuge,
my shield[b] and the horn[c] of my salvation, my stronghold.

3 I called to the LORD, who is worthy of praise,
and I have been saved from my enemies.

4 The cords of death entangled me;
the torrents of destruction overwhelmed me.

5 The cords of the grave coiled around me;
the snares of death confronted me.

6 In my distress I called to the LORD;
I cried to my God for help.
From his temple he heard my voice;
my cry came before him, into his ears.

7 The earth trembled and quaked,
and the foundations of the mountains shook;
they trembled because he was angry.

8 Smoke rose from his nostrils;
consuming fire came from his mouth,
burning coals blazed out of it.

9 He parted the heavens and came down;
dark clouds were under his feet.

10 He mounted the cherubim and flew;
he soared on the wings of the wind.

11 He made darkness his covering, his canopy around
him –the dark rain clouds of the sky.

12 Out of the brightness of his presence clouds
advanced,with hailstones and bolts of lightning.

13 The LORD thundered from heaven;
the voice of the Most High resounded.

14 He shot his arrows and scattered the enemy,
with great bolts of lightning he routed them.

15 The valleys of the sea were exposed
and the foundations of the earth laid bare
at your rebuke, LORD,
at the blast of breath from your nostrils.

16 He reached down from on high and took hold of
me; he drew me out of deep waters.

17 He rescued me from my powerful enemy,
from my foes, who were too strong for me.

18 They confronted me in the day of my disaster,
but the LORD was my support.

19 He brought me out into a spacious place;
he rescued me because he delighted in me.

20 The LORD has dealt with me according to my
righteousness; according to the cleanness of my
hands he has rewarded me.\

21 For I have kept the ways of the LORD;
I am not guilty of turning from my God.

22 All his laws are before me;
I have not turned away from his decrees.

23 I have been blameless before him
and have kept myself from sin.

24 The LORD has rewarded me according to my
righteousness, according to the cleanness of my
hands in his sight.

25 To the faithful you show yourself faithful,
to the blameless you show yourself blameless,

26 to the pure you show yourself pure,
but to the devious you show yourself shrewd.

27 You save the humble
but bring low those whose eyes are haughty.

28 You, LORD, keep my lamp burning;
my God turns my darkness into light.

29 With your help I can advance against a troop;
with my God I can scale a wall.

30 As for God, his way is perfect:
the LORD's word is flawless;
he shields all who take refuge in him.\

31 For who is God besides the LORD?
And who is the Rock except our God?

32 It is God who arms me with strength
and keeps my way secure.

33 He makes my feet like the feet of a deer;
he causes me to stand on the heights.

34 He trains my hands for battle;
my arms can bend a bow of bronze.

35 You make your saving help my shield,
and your right hand sustains me;
your help has made me great.

36 You provide a broad path for my feet,
so that my ankles do not give way.

37 I pursued my enemies and overtook them;
I did not turn back till they were destroyed.

38 I crushed them so that they could not rise;
they fell beneath my feet.

39 You armed me with strength for battle;
you humbled my adversaries before me.

40 You made my enemies turn their backs in flight,
and I destroyed my foes.

41 They cried for help, but there was no one to save
them – to the LORD, but he did not answer.

42 I beat them as fine as windblown dust;
I trampled them[f] like mud in the streets.

43 You have delivered me from the attacks of the
people; you have made me the head of nations.
People I did not know now serve me,

44 foreigners cower before me;
as soon as they hear of me, they obey me.

45 They all lose heart;
they come trembling from their strongholds.

46 The LORD lives! Praise be to my Rock!
Exalted be God my Saviour!

> 47 He is the God who avenges me,
> who subdues nations under me,
>
> 48 who saves me from my enemies.
> You exalted me above my foes;
> from a violent man you rescued me.
>
> 49 Therefore I will praise you, LORD, among the
> nations; I will sing the praises of your name.
>
> 50 He gives his king great victories;
> he shows unfailing love to his anointed,
> to David and to his descendants forever.

As we proclaimed this promise from God over our family, the sky darkened just as if the Lord was so angry, he was indeed, bowing the heavens and coming down with thick darkness under His feet. Hidden in the darkness of the clouds He sent forth hailstones and lightening. Outside of our home, we saw the strike of the lightening and the sound of thunder and then the crashing sound of a hailstone storm falling from the sky.

We were riding the heights of the victory in that moment; our confidence growing as we confessed God's Word! The storm adding to the momentum of our faith. Finally the storm began to dissipate and we came peacefully into a state of thanksgiving and praise.

After we finished our time together I went outside to see if we really did have hail stones fall, and right by our front door step I scooped up a handful of large balls of frozen Ice. I smiled and thanked God.

It was a few years later in 2016 when I shared the photograph of my hand holding the hailstones to my brother. He stared at the photograph in disbelief and asked me about the significance of the hail stones. I read out loud to him Psalm 18 and he wept. He then shared a time in his life years earlier where he came near to death, he was able to walk away from the danger and as he did so there came a mighty hail storm as if the Lord was saying "I have come to rescue you and I will save you. I am angry with those who would try to take your life and now trust that as My child I have rescued you out of the hands of death.

CHAPTER 9

Entering Rest- A new way of life

From that time, there was a shift in our thinking. We could see a light at the end of this very dark tunnel. To be honest, as it was now early December, I was just counting the days till we closed the business. I did keep very close to the Lord and began to look forward to quiet times with Him. I began to think about a certain man in our church family; it was as if God was trying to get my attention to connect with this man. He was, and still is, a wonderful man of God who works tirelessly for vulnerable people in our city.

"Maybe we could work for him Father?" I just wanted to get far away from just a job trying to earn big money and I also just wanted to not 'do' anything. Hugh and I were battered; we were battle weary and had been out in the cold too long.

As it happened, I was invited to the ladies group which was facilitated by the church. The group is held for women who are lonely; who haven't been cherished throughout their lives and looking to rebuild a life based on love and friendship. I had spoken a few times in the group and the pastor wanted to thank me by way of joining them for Christmas lunch. This centre was where the church congregated, at that time, on a Sunday. There is also a café.

As I was on my way to the centre, I asked God, that if he really was directing me by the Holy Spirit to this man called Marvin whom he had put on my heart, then let him not only be in the café on the day I was going for the lunch, but that he would also have time to talk to me!

As I arrived and walked into the café, sure enough, there he was. I went over to him and said,

"Hi Marvin, I wonder if you have a few spare minutes for a quick chat?"

"Yes of course I have", he said.

I sat down at his table and told him that the Lord had put him on my heart, not as a concern, but that I felt God was directing me to talk to him.

We chatted about the predicament Hugh and I were in and he said he couldn't offer us any paid work as there was no money in the pot but that there was plenty of voluntary work.

I told him we needed some money to live. Marvin said,

"Look, why not join us and our family for lunch on Christmas Eve?"

I said I would be able to but Hugh would still be working in the restaurant. So on Christmas Eve I went to see Marvin and his family for lunch. It was lovely to meet his family, but there was still no sense as to why God had been directing me to him.

However, on Christmas morning my text message alert sounded and it was a message from Marvin. He had attended the Christmas Eve carol service the previous evening and was told by the Café manager that one of his staff had left. There was a vacancy in the café and it would need someone to start straight after the New Year. If I got the position, it would mean I would work five days a week; I was so excited and just knew this was from the Lord. I knew I wasn't ready to go into another demanding job; I had lost my energy, my confidence and I just wanted a quiet, simple life! I was going to apply then wait to see if I would be successful.

On Christmas day, Hugh and I and the staff at the restaurant, all knew this would be the last shift. The day went well in business terms but it was a very strange day. Most of the customers seemed miserable and awkward and I could not wait for the last customers to leave. Once they left, we emptied the till with our takings to pay the staff. After that, there wasn't a penny left. We walked away with nothing. It was a painful time.

I was successful in getting the post as Deputy Manager at the Café. Hugh started to look for work. He decided he would go and have a chat with Marvin and see if there was any voluntary work he could do. As Marvin had explained to me, there was no paid work because there wasn't any spare money for an extra salary at the charity he was overseeing. Hugh and I discussed the matter and we both agreed that after coming out of a very dry and dark place spiritually, we were going to trust in the Lord completely! We prayed,

"Lord, we thank you for our work. We trust that even though Hugh is working voluntary, that you would provide all our needs."

We had lost all our savings and it felt we couldn't drop any further down; we were at rock bottom. But the strange thing was, it also felt very liberating, the fact that we had nothing to lose!

I began working in the café; it was like balm to my soul. I was so battered by my time at the restaurant, yet even though only one week had gone by, I felt as if the restaurant was a million miles away. As I worked the short days in the week and having weekends free I began to relax and enjoy the delights of working without the pressure of worrying about so many things that had stolen my joy in the restaurant.

As I worked, I was so in love with God. He had provided me with such freedom and love! I was overwhelmed! He had brought me back into my broad place because He loves me. I have always worn my faith on my sleeve and now, I was so thankful for coming through this challenging time and being delivered from it. I was on fire for the

Lord! People came into the café and I would pray with them. Miracles of healing and love were taking place and God was divinely blessing the work in the kitchen. Joanne my manager at the time, and I, were like a small dynamic duo; she described us as a 'Mary and Martha' couple. She would be cooking and beavering away and I would keep popping out into the café to pray for someone who had been blown in by the Holy Spirit looking to get a healing balm touch from the Lord. We literally fed people spiritually and physically. One thing about the church we attended, is that it had a huge heart for broken people and we were able to feed many people on the practical side with food but we were also able to feed them spiritually.

We realised in the school holidays that there would be many children who would not get a decent meal during holiday times like they do at school, so we decided to join together with a local supplier and offer a free breakfast club. There was so much goodwill from many people to help and donate food and through that small event we met some lovely people who have now been baptised and have joined our church family.

Hugh had been shadowing Marvin's position at the local Foodbank for eight months in order to understand his work and to be able to relieve Marvin of tasks that took up a lot of his time. This allowed Marvin the opportunity to extend his energies into other productive activities. Hugh in time was given the post as 'Operations Manager' for the Foodbank. This ministry is still to this day, climbing from strength to strength, as the food bank team work hard, meeting the growing needs of many in poverty.

CHAPTER 10

Stepping into the breach

In mid-2014 I had been getting the same word from the Lord telling me God was opening new doors for me. I became aware of this happening. I was in the café but sensing that God was about to move me into a new place.

In late April 2015, I was aware that over the past six months or more, I had been contacted by several women who were alone and lonely. Women who were just staying in their homes and not having the confidence or energy to leave their homes. They each in turn sought me out and asked me to come and pray with them. As I visited each woman, I realised some of their problems were so big, and out of all our control I wasn't sure how I was able to help naturally. However on one occasion, I was visiting a woman who was very depressed and sick. Her home was cold and she was living in one room. I asked her if she would pray with me and she said yes. As we prayed, I opened my eyes to look at her face. There was such an earnest look of devotion to God as she sat there praying. My heart went out to her, and when I left her and sat in my car, I cried.

"Lord, I'm feeling so helpless here what can I do?"

"Pray that's what I want you to do" He said

So I went every week to visit her and prayed. She began to get her health back and she also started coming to some of the women's groups at the church. I decided after much prayer to step out in faith. I set up a small project called 'Homebound', which has two meanings, one being bound up at home but also home bound toward the truth that sets them free. This comes out of a time when I too was Homebound. It was at the time when Stuart was in prison and I was so depressed I couldn't work properly and my debts were rising as my health deteriorated. I stayed at home, lost all of my confidence and just existed. Having experienced being homebound I have a heart for women who for one reason or another are imprisoned in their own homes not knowing how to get out of the situation.

I left the Café and started to work voluntarily as pastoral outreach to these women. The project 'Homebound' is a powerful ministry.

One day in early May 2015 just after I left the café work, I met a lady who had come into the country as an asylum seeker. She had just been given leave to remain in the country and as such had moved from the temporary accommodation that the government provide for most asylum seekers until they get their status in the UK. I knew her as part of our church family and she asked me what I was doing as she had not seen me in the café recently. I told her about the project I had set up and she told me about the woman that had moved into the house she had just left, that she was an asylum seeker from Syria. She told me that the woman was also eight months pregnant and she had no family with her. She then gave me the number for the landlord and told me to call him. He spoke a bit of Arabic and said he would let the woman know I would be coming to visit her.

I arrived at her home on May 9th 2015. I knocked the door and a small heavily pregnant woman appeared. There was a sadness to her eyes as she beckoned me in. I told her in slow English that my name was Debbie. She smiled a weak smile. I sat in the poorly furnished room, at least it was warm and dry. She gave me a number and I realised that this was the number of an interpreter who would speak English and Arabic. His name was Abdul. He spoke to this lady who is called Shabana. She told him that she wanted a lift to the hospital on the Monday morning, as she was booked in for a Caesarean section. I asked if she would need help and Abdul said there would be someone with her.

I went and bought food for her. I discovered that she had a family in Crete. They had all come on the dangerous journey from Syria and she was pregnant. Her children had suffered badly on the boat and one of her little girls had been in hospital for nine weeks after the boat journey. Shabana was able to get a flight to the UK and seek Asylum. There was no money for her family to come. She had been here on her own for seven months.

I took her early on the Monday morning to the hospital. There was no women to support her, I discovered through the Arabic surgeon – she was completely on her own. I noticed her shaking as they prepared her for surgery. She was the same age as my eldest daughter Catherine. I gently took her hand and squeezed it smiling at her with comfort.

"Oh Lord am I really able to support this young woman and be present at the birth of her new baby, even though I've known her two days.

I heard the Lord clearly say to me,

"I have given you open doors that no one can shut"

I remembered back to the scripture in Isaiah 22:22.

Then I will set the key of the house of David on his shoulder, when he opens no one will shut and when he shuts no one will open. He had indeed opened this door for me.

Little baby Adam was born and I held him for two hours while his mother had her surgery. There were complications. I prayed over Adam and I prayed over the mother. How blessed was I to be the birth partner of a stranger in our land! I held baby Adam up to Shabana's face as she was still being operated on, tears trickled down her face. Nothing needed to be said.

Miracle after miracle happened. God graciously blessed my work with Shabana.

I supported her as she was being evicted from the government house four days after giving birth. The local council housed her as an emergency in a small hotel. She found favor with the receptionist who gave her one of the best rooms and kept her eye on her. Meantime she had no money, so I was able to get her money and food.

I asked her why she was sad. I had discovered a translator app and we got by with that when we had no interpreter. We had become good friends, and I began to see her laugh and smile at some of my musings. She allowed me to pray over her and the baby when they got sick. God always healed them.

We prayed about her four children left in Crete with her husband, she so badly wanted them home. The cost through a solicitor was going to cost at least a thousand pounds, and a wait of over a year! I decided to try and sort it out. I contacted a charity I had volunteered for when we were living in the New Forest. They support trafficked women and children and work with refugees on immigration issues and licensed to do this work. I got some great support with them and also with the help of Abdul the interpreter we were able to gather all the information needed for a family reunion. The paper work had to be sent to Athens, but who would I send it to?

I was concerned these important documents would get lost and they were needed by Shabana's husband when they went for their interview at the visa office in Athens.

"Oh Lord who shall I send these papers to?" I prayed one day.

As the family were living rough we were not sure where to send the papers to. God however told me very clearly to wait.

The interview date was looming and I said to the Lord,

"Lord the date is coming soon we need to send the papers."

I heard nothing so I waited.

I decided that if I hadn't heard anything by the coming Saturday that I would find a courier in Athens and take a risk to send the papers there.

Saturday morning at 8 am I got a text message;

"Hi Debbie you don't know me, my name is Katy, I have been given your number by the Syrian family and they said you are helping the wife Shabana. Can we speak?

I couldn't believe it. I called the number and got through to a British lady called Katy who lives in Crete, a school teacher she had been teaching the children and helping to support Shabana's family. I sent the papers by courier to her address. She was able to take the family on the two hour journey to the docks and then they got on a boat on a nine hour journey to Athens. It sounds like a 007 movie, but this little family were frightened. They had their appointments with the Visa office, and then they had to make the journey back to Crete. Ten days later their visas were ready to allow them to join Shabana on the family reunion visa into the UK. I borrowed the church min-bus and together with Shabana and a friend we drove to the Airport to fetch the children and the husband, it was 31st August 2015 only three months after I had met Shabana for the first time. A miracle! People had kindly donated most of the airfare. We were very blessed.

Shabana was breast feeding the baby in the rest room at the airport when the family finally appeared. I had only seen photographs of them and when they appeared it was I who ran to meet them calling out their names. We embraced and the children hugged me. It was as if I'd known them all my life.

The scene, after a year apart, seeing this family reunited was I have to say heart lifting and I give all honour and glory to God who made it happen.

As my work developed people sent cheques in the post to support the work I was doing. A couple I know even donated money each month toward helping Hugh and I as we were only getting his small wage. However God was great and we were blessed in so many other ways that this was an incredible time.

By the end of October 2015 I arranged a meeting with a lady from the council to discuss with her the project and the work with the refugees, I was now working with four other asylum seekers, all women alone at home, some with young children. Each one of their stories was heart wrenching. I realised that I was able to delegate the work and realised that God had used my talent of networking and gathering resourceful people to support. After this meeting I got an email to reveal my current post working with refugees coming into the UK on humanitarian protection. I decided to take up the post and applied successfully for this role. I have been able to train more in this field to discover efficient ways of responding to refugees and migrants in the UK.

As I work in each ministry balancing this work, I am working towards the fullness of my calling.

CHAPTER 11

Revelation of my Father

Life was settling down and I asked the Lord to allow us time to rest before the next upgrade. It was at this time that the Holy Spirit gently reminded me that I had unfinished business regarding the identity and relationship with my earthly father. My Mum had told me when I was in my late thirties that my biological father was not the man I had always been told was. The man whom I thought was my dad died when I was a little girl. He had never been a loving father to me and maybe because he died when I was seven, I wasn't really upset about his passing. I can recall being more upset about my mum's tears at the church service mass that was held the evening before his funeral.

As I've written earlier in the book, my mum then married Jack who was the best father I could wish for, and I miss him dearly. I would love to tell him how I feel and thank him for his care and love for us; he was truly a wonderful servant-hearted man.

In my late thirties, having come through the divorce from my first husband and facing the challenges of my second husbands controlling lifestyle, I had come to a time of struggling with a light depression. In an attempt to understand what was wrong, I began to look back over my life and look at all the significant relationships that had influenced my life. I worked through my life with my first dad who died when I was a child. Then having Jack as my step dad and who being a lot older than mum was more of a loving grandfather figure in my young life. As I looked at the role of my first husband I could begin to see clearly that he was the 'father figure' that I had been searching for. When we divorced some fifteen years later, it was for me a realisation that as a father figure I had naturally grown up and wanted to leave home. Searching for peace I began to ask my siblings why I felt different. I also decided to speak to my mum and ask her about my father. I cried to her. I told her how I felt I needed to forgive my first dad as I never really liked the way he treated me or mum.

(He was always fighting with mum and that scared me). I was surprised when mum suddenly revealed a secret.

"Well he is not your dad Debra, your father is a man called David." I could tell she felt uncomfortable as she unfolded the story of how they had met and dated for over three years. Both being married to another, they kept their secret under wraps. That was until in 1962 she fell pregnant with me and I was born in June 1963. David and mums relationship cooled after my birth. Mum said he came to see me one night when he knew my first dad was at the pub. I was asleep apparently in my pram. After this David made a decision and that was to move his family to South Africa.

I cast my mind back recalling a conversation a few years before this revelation from mum, I'd had with one of my sisters. I had asked her if we really had the same dad. There had been something within me that made me strongly feel different from the others and I wanted to get to the bottom of this concern. My sister said she didn't think we did have the same dad as she, being the eldest remembered when I was born my dad said,

"She's not one of mine; she's too beautiful to be mine".

I remembered that my mum and dad's marriage was always rocky; they would end up in the most terrible fights and I was there to witness them; always taking my mum's side. When mum fell pregnant with me it was a shock to her, and she did regret that she was pregnant at the time of her finding out she was. Spiritually even though I was still in the womb it was another rejection. My dad David rejected me out of fear of the truth being revealed, with the chance that his other family would find out about me.

Now at the age of thirty-nine my mum admitted to me that I did indeed have a different biological father than that of my siblings.

Mum also told me that David had two children. I had another sister and a brother!

In my fortieth year, after finding out the details of my biological father, I decided to search for him. I began to look for him on the internet and found a man of his name and roughly the same age who was the CEO of a huge South African company. There were no pictures and I shied away from looking further, but I did begin to check the birth records and found him, his parents and siblings. I also found his marriage certificate and birth of his daughter, Deborah! My elder sister! With the same name as me! I asked mum why she had called me by the same name and she said it was always to remind David that he had another daughter called Debra!

In 2010 and well into my new identity as a born again follower of Jesus, I decided to resurrect my search and found that the CEO I thought was my dad was now in a photo gallery of the company I thought he worked at. The man in question had black skin and seemed to be of African or Caribbean heritage, and I firmly believed the chances of him being my father were pretty slim.

I began to search the worldwide web again and this time, with the advancements in technology and my new facts and details, I discovered my father's whereabouts, He was living in New York! I decided to write to him rather than phone him. I prayed over the letter and sent it off. I put in my email address and it wasn't long before I got a response on my email. He was confused and wanted to know how I knew so much about him. We exchanged many emails over the months. However after hearing his story and he, mine, the trail suddenly went cold. He stopped responding to the emails and I realised he wasn't happy about staying in contact with me. Another rejection, but this time I could handle it. Instead of feeling like a victim I knew I had discovered my true Father and been given a 'Love' that surpasses all understanding, the love of my heavenly Father! I prayed David would be blessed in his life and sorry he had missed out on meeting such a wonderful daughter.

In Peace I carried on through life in my new identity in God as my Father.

One day in 2011, David's email address was hacked with an advert for a pharmaceutical drug and his email address list was sent to me with a link for this drug! I noticed there was a 'Deborah' on the email. I had searched for her name a few times and this woman's name had come up. She was the Head of an International organisation. I held this information for long time. I was worried about the impact it may have on her life and I was worried that my contacting her would cause some trouble. I prayed and asked the Lord to reveal the right time for me to contact her. In 2014, I decided to pluck up the courage to email her and tentatively sent an email in which I asked her if she was the Deborah who was born in my hometown, in this certain year, revealing her mother's name and saying if she had a dad called David? I also named her brother Liam, a man my mother had mentioned.

She emailed back and confirmed she was indeed that girl and I knew I had just found the sister I had never met before! We emailed back and forth and eventually Debs called me and we chatted on the phone. She told me we had a younger brother as well as the older brother, and I was delighted to know that I had another brother.

In August 2014, Debs was coming to the UK and we finally arranged to meet. Our first meeting was in a local hotel and when I saw her I loved her straight away! It was like I was looking at myself. She has the same huge smile as me and when in her company her enigmatic charm spreads to everyone in her company! Debs popped up to Scotland for a trip then returned to see us once again. We met at a lovely old pub in Berkswell. We spent the day there and this time she brought her handsome son with her and I met my nephew for the first time. Each being huge Rugby fans, Hugh and our nephew chatted away while Debs and I decided we would go out into the pub garden and call 'our' dad!

I was very nervous and when she announced to him I was with her and she was handing the phone over to me, I was really nervous. I was about to speak to my dad in person for the first time ever!!!

I cried as we spoke; this was an amazing moment for me. Dad spoke softly on the phone and at one point he said *"You sound so English!"*

"That's because I live in England!" I laughed.

We ended our phone call with promises to keep in touch and I have made a few calls to him over in New York. I know I will get to meet my dad face to face at some stage in the near future.

CHAPTER 12

Restoration So what's it all about?

In the bible God changes names of people when there is about to be a significant move of God in their spirit, Abraham and Sarah, Jacob and Peter all had names changed. Why did God choose new names for some people? The Bible doesn't give us His reasons, but perhaps it was to let them know they were destined for a new mission in life. The new name was a way to let them in on the divine plan and also to assure them that God's plan would be fulfilled in them.

As I was reading a book recently, the author explains that we all have a life message to share with others. He explains that sometimes we need to look in the familiar places where God might speak to us.

Where better than His word to start in the familiar. I took this advice and began to think about what I'd read the very first time I opened the Bible. Of course it was as I described earlier in the book where God revealed immediately the answer to my question,

"If all this is true God reveal it to me now" as I randomly opened the bible.

And as I opened the book there in front of me was God's beautiful words which I felt were at that time very personal to me; Judges 5:12

"Awake Awake Deborah Awake and sing a song."

I felt compelled to read the chapters about Deborah and it was so amazing how God spoke to me about my life message, my calling.

Deborah was anointed by God to be a Judge over Israel, she was also a prophetess with an ability to discern the mind and purpose of God and declare it to others. She was an agitator, raising the people of God to fight for their inheritance.

Sitting in my garden in the morning sunshine I was reflecting on this mighty woman of God. I suddenly became aware of a Bee inside one of the flowers, as I looked closer the Bee was drinking the nectar from the tiny tendrils inside the flower. I felt a real sense of the Holy Spirit revealing something to me.

I decided to study the Bee, I already knew that the Hebrew meaning of the name Deborah was the Bee. I read that the Bee ranks amongst the highest intelligence, as much as Deborah stands out as the wisest of all the Old Testament women.

The Bee on collecting the nectar then shares this nectar with another Bee from the same hive, which allows the water to reduce from the nectar and the nectar becomes like liquid gold, more concentrated and richer, this is then taken back to the hive for feeding the family. When the Bees find a good supply of nectar and pollen, they go back to their hive family and doing a dance, wiggling their bodies to lead the family to the harvest of flower fruits.

I began to understand that as my heavenly Father was changing me and allowing my new Spirit to emerge He also changed my name spiritually. I began to step into the new anointed role of Deborah. Taking the word of God, (the nectar) meditating, then sharing with others the revelations that come from this word. Sharing experiences with others allows us to take away watered down versions and allows the Holy Spirit to reveal the pure nectar of His Word. I always work to reveal to others where the treasure of this fruit lies so that we can work together to glean the fruits of the word to ourselves and to others.

By doing this we can all grow in our intimate relationship with God and each other.

> Ephesians 2:21-22
>
> *In Him the whole building is fitted together and grows into a holy temple in the Lord. And in Him you too are being built together into a dwelling place for God in His Spirit.*

The reason that God chose Deborah to be this mighty woman of God was that she was PREPARED to come out of her comfort zone, and with courage and wisdom rule and reign over Israel for over forty years.

We can all step into our life calling and begin to ask God to reveal his anointing gifting's on our life.

(See the web site for more details of the course that runs alongside this book to help you discover your calling and gifting's)

In the story in Judges, Deborah is married to a man called Lapidoth. His name means illuminator and I believe part of my life message is to encourage men to be the man that God created them to be. I believe so much that our men need to rise up. Deborah stood with her man, and also commanded the leader of the army, Barak to 'Rise Up'. I believe as women we need to be encouraging our men and allowing them to feel validated and respected, in doing so they will become 'great fathers, sons and husbands.' Our children will be brought up with stability and a God given template as to how family life should be. It may seem a long way off in today's world but we must start somewhere. When I met my husband Hugh, he was broken in many ways. It took us time to be the married couple we are today. We have now become as one, enmeshed into our marriage where there is love and mutual respect. I supported Hugh to 'Rise Up' and be the man God created him to be.

In doing so the love he gives me allows me to be the great woman God created me to be.

I began to understand that we had both come from a broken place of rejection, and through our healing we now have an amazing ministry as a mother and father to many.

Hugh works with many men to support and enable them to become the great men God called them to be, and I likewise with the wonderful women I meet.

This is nectar, this is the dance, and this is me awake and ready to reveal to others how much our Father Loves us, all of us!

Take your brokenness and give it to Jesus, speak to him as if you are having a normal conversation with a friend and tell him all your concerns and worries. Then ask him to teach you His ways and allow him to lead you into the new life He has for you.

Awake Awake Deborah and Sing!

ABOUT THE AUTHOR

Debra McNeill B.A (Hons) Youth and Community & Applied Theology

Debra McNeill has worked pastoring young people, children and families, from local communities, rehabilitation centres, in her own therapy business, and more recently with a project called 'Home Bound' where she pastors women who for many reasons were lonely at home and unable to face the outside world. Debra has worked in these arenas for over 20 years, supporting and enabling others to overcome adversity in their lives and become people who can go forwards with confidence and with the freedom from past damaging experiences.

Debra is married to Hugh and together they have four daughters and a granddaughter.

They live in a small village in England.

As part of her calling, Debra is currently working with refugees from war torn countries such as Syria and Afghanistan, enabling these families to resettle into the UK on Humanitarian Grounds.

This is Debra's first book which she has felt was being drawn from her by her heavenly Father so that others whose experiences are similar to Debra's old life styles may understand the Hope that is there for them.

Debra is currently offering a life style on line and event courses to enable others to move towards that Hope and live a life filled with peace love and joy.

For more information please go to her website www.debramcneill.com